MANAGEMENT TOOLS
FOR EVERYONE:
Twenty Analytical Techniques
That Are Easy to Learn
and Valuable to Know

MANAGEMENT TOOLS FOR EVERYONE:

Twenty Analytical Techniques That Are Easy to Learn and Valuable to Know

Steve M. Erickson

PBI
a petrocelli book
new york / princeton

Designed by Diane Backes
Typesetting by Backes Graphics

Library of Congress Cataloging in Publication Data

Erickson, Steve M.
  Management tools for everyone.

  Includes index.
  1. Management. I. Title
HD31.E74   658   81-5136
ISBN 0-89433-131-0   AACR2

Contents

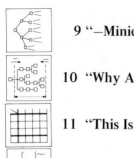

Introduction

During the past several years, I've become slowly aware of a growing tendency for clients and groups with whom I work to ask for "models." At first I didn't understand what they were talking about, or why they were making the request. Gradually, as I analyzed the situations which generated this search for models, I realized that the request reflected a need to visualize . . . a need to capture graphically the interwoven issues we were facing.

Once this insight penetrated my somewhat stubborn skull, I began to ask for and to seek models myself. Soon I achieved a second insight: that models which assist conceptualization are important communication and management tools.

It is this aspect of modeling that Steve M. Erickson has developed: in Steve's analysis, models are indeed *Management Tools For Everyone.* He has assembled, explained and described applications for twenty such analytical techniques. (Fortunately, every one of the twenty has a graphic manifestation, so we can *see* what they are and how they work—and more importantly, how they might work for us).

From my early frustrations in trying to develop models, and my later deeper despair in trying to comprehend modeling theory, I was frankly skeptical of a book compiling twenty such tools! But I found that it was fun to read the manuscript: it uses many solid graphic techniques and titles that work much like those in Information Mapping, and quotations that add spice and sense to the content. It has chapter outlines that are pictures—not outlines at all. The examples which explain the model/tools are simple and lifelike without being simplistic. I found them to be like the book itself: just direct and naive enough to be refreshing and helpful.

Dugan Laird

Acknowledgments

Many individuals have given you, the reader, this book through their personal support and toil. Herman McDaniel and Orlando Petrocelli, receptive to the basic idea, made this publication possible. Donna Moore provided sustaining encouragement throughout the effort and invaluably assisted in ensuring clarity of my exposition. Betty Fine gave many hours of skillful secretarial support. Generously, Dugan Laird reviewed the work. Help also came from Hudson Henry, Chris Bender, and Nancy Harper. And no less importantly, Deanna Erickson contributed understanding and enduring patience—the cement that held the pieces together. I am gratefully indebted to all these many friends.

Steve M. Erickson

Preface

Recent research reveals a significant distinction between the two hemispheres of the human brain. The left hemisphere is directly associated with activities that are logical, analytical, or sequential. In contrast, the right hemisphere directs intuitive, artistic, or holistic activities. Depending on the activity that consumes our attention at any given moment, the appropriate hemisphere is actively engaged, whereas the other remains relatively passive.

The same research concludes that, as an individual, each of us has a natural dominance of one hemisphere (right or left) over the other. Hence each of us has somewhat lopsidely cultivated a prominence of either intuitive perception or logical reasoning. One individual may be basically "left-brained" (that is, logical), whereas another may be "right-brained" (intuitive).

All this is said to illustrate that there are fundamental differences in the mental approach of people. We should not value either the "intuitive" or the "logical" over the other; both are powerful gifts of nature, and each has its special value. How resplendent it would be if we were equally gifted in both. Yet we *can* increase our faculties in both areas.

This book is a compendium of analytical tools typically found in the broad field known as *management*. Readers of either right- or left-brained disposition should find these tools immensely helpful in improving their analytical abilities. In fact the book was specifically written to make easy learning of these logic tools for intuitive people. Here, in one source, are twenty tools of logic (taken from such disciplines as data processing, industrial engineering, and public-program management). They were chosen because over the years each has proved useful. Because these tools are in chart form, all are definitive and can be understood quickly.

The concepts underlying each tool have been simplified—stripped of their "bells and whistles"—and reduced to their essential elements. Even the examples are simplistic. Regardless of occupation or organizational position, each reader should find many of the techniques personally useful.

Because most of us are, in one way or another, in an organizational environment, each tool is presented in an organizational context. The reader, however, will undoubtedly discover applicability to personal affairs.

By its structure, the book reflects that some readers seek to learn from it, whereas others merely wish to use the book as a reference. Many guides are included, which should help you quickly find and adapt the ideas found in this book to your interests.

If our brain is "lopsided" this book is equally so, for it focuses entirely upon the logical, the rational. It does so without apology, assuming that the reader will apply its suggested approaches with artful skill and intuition. "Physicists have 'proved' rationally, that our rational ideas about the world in which we live are profoundly deficient."[1] The tools in this book are very useful, yet to rely on any or all of them solely is both simplistic and unwise. Use them to augment—not substitute for—your intuition and reason. Each tool is only *one* answer, and "any answer is only a point of view. A point of view itself is limiting. To 'understand' something is to give up some other way of conceiving (of) it."[2] Seek the wisdom needed to balance what the tools appear to say.

Logic is a large drawer, containing some needful instruments, and many which are superfluous . . . A wise man will look into it for two purposes, to avail himself of those instruments that are really useful, and to admire the ingenuity with which those that are not so assorted and arranged.

Caleb C. Colton (1780-1832)

---

1. *Gary Zukav, *The Dancing Wu Li Masters*, New York: William Morrow, 1979, p. 327; reprinted with permission from William Morrow, Inc.
2. Zukav, ibid. p. 327.

This book is designed to be a tool-box, a drawer of needful instruments. The book is a compendium of analytical tools—usefully selected for their utility and presented straightforwardly for easy learning.

Steve M. Erickson

1

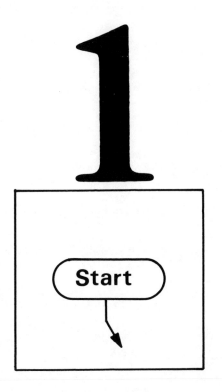

"Everybody Starts Here"

OUTLINE
OF
CHAPTER
ONE

Overview of
This Book

AN OVERVIEW { structure of the book
structure of the chapters

ITS VALUE { an illustration

HOW TO USE
THIS BOOK { two kinds of use
three approaches

The Tools

WHAT ARE THEY? { four examples

THE VALUE OF
THE TOOLS { applications
advantages

USING THE TOOLS { scientific method
advice

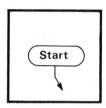

When a thing is intelligible you have a sense of participation; when a thing is unintelligible you have a sense of estrangement.— If the mind cannot bring to the world a set.... or, shall we say, a tool-box— of powerful ideas, the world must appear to it as a chaos, a mass of unrelated phenomena, of meaningless events.

E. F. Schumacher*

An Overview of This Book

This book is a tool box of twenty analytical tools that have not been put in one box before. Traditionally, these tools have been used to solve management problems. Like any tool, however, they lend themselves to a variety of uses. They can prove useful, both in your personal life and in an organizational setting. Each tool is easy to grasp, for all revolve around some form of chart.

Individual chapters are devoted to a particular analytical technique or to several techniques if they are closely related. Generally speaking, the various tools are not related to one another any more than a saw is related to a hammer. Thus there is little continuity among chapters. Each chapter, does, however, provide the basics first and then the refinements. Each chapter begins with an outline.

Imagine an ordinary person wishing to make life more purposeful (out of what the Chinese philosophers call the "confusion of ten-thousand things"). Our ordinary person takes out paper and pen to

*E. F. Schumacher, *Small Is Beautiful*, New York: Harper and Row, 1975, p. 84. Reprinted with permission of Harper and Row, Inc.

create a diagram reflecting personal values. That diagram attempts to relate daily objectives and activities in such a way that they will be meaningful. Every item relates to the others, as follows: *why* an objective is pursued is explained by a higher purpose to the *left*; *how* an objective can be achieved is portrayed by those to the *right*. Figure 1.1 shows an incomplete portion of the diagram. Focus on the relationship connecting the boxes in the shaded area.

The scenario is somewhat unrealistic. Most of us search for meaning, though few are as structured as this. Admittedly, to infer that one can enjoy life by learning analytical tools may sound absurd. When we include the intervening pieces, however, the connection becomes clearer. Read the chart from right to left, and it will explain one way that these tools can be of value to you.

The tools help us solve logic problems, for example, by improving procedures, evaluating alternatives, and making decisions. To quote E. F. Schumacher again, "problems which can be solved by logic are man's most useful invention . . . . When they have been solved, the solution can be written down and passed on to others who can apply it without needing to reproduce the mental effort necessary to find it."*

How to Use This Book

Perhaps you are reading this to *learn* new and useful techniques. At some later time, after exposure to these tools, you may wish to refresh your knowledge, in which case you will want to *refer* to the appropriate section for information. Many aids are included to assist your use of this book, for both purposes—learning and referencing. The figures below will help you. Taken together, Figure 1.2 and 1.3 and tables 1.1 and 1.2 form a self-explanatory guide to the effective use of this book, to meet your particular needs.

The tools

Now, just what are these "analytical tools"? Are they complex and formidable? No, they are neither complex nor formidable. Without a formal explanation, you have already become familiar with four of them. Let's examine each more closely.

---

*Schumacher, ibid.

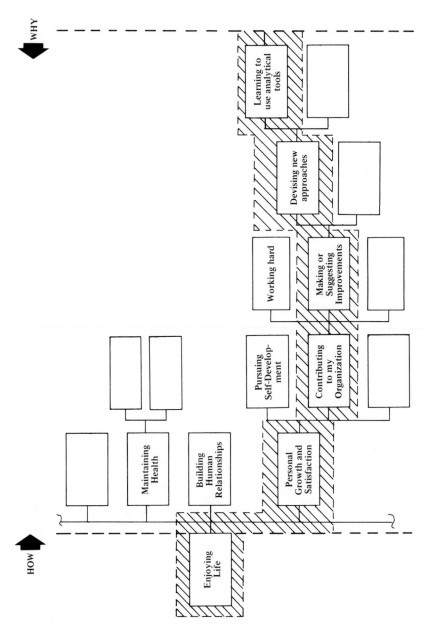

FIGURE 1.1: Enjoying life

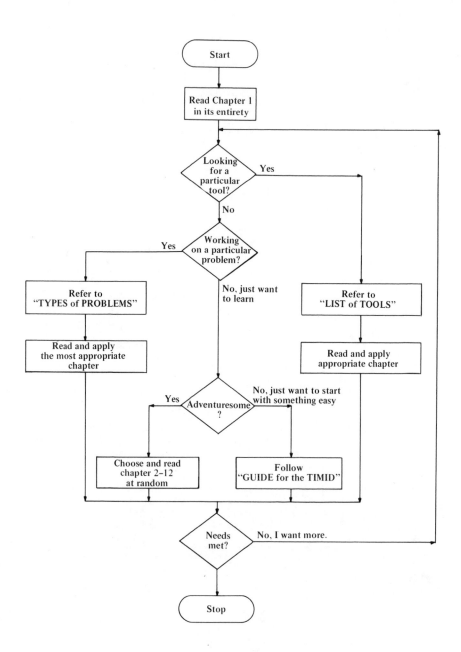

FIGURE 1.2: How to use this book.

TABLE 1.1: *List of tools*

Figure 1.1, "Enjoying Life," is described as the conscious effort to create a structured perspective of one's life. The technique used is called a FAST diagram. It visually portrays the hierarchical relationship of all the elements in the boxes. Reading from left to right, we see *how* to implement our goal, which is on the far left. Reading in the reverse direction, right to left, we see the progressively larger motivations that underlie *why* an objective or task is done. The essence of this analytical tool should be clear to you without reading Chapter 10.

Figure 1.2, "How to Use This Book," directs the reader to the most appropriate approach to using this book in order to meet the reader's specific needs. The diagram is an example of an ADP flowchart, an analytical tool that graphically displays the sequence of steps in a process for all the various conditions that may arise.

A different technique, called a Warnier Diagram, is shown in Table 1.2 It displays the hierarchical relationship of the many elements of a

TABLE 1.2: *Types of problems*

TYPE OF PROBLEM			
Defining A Problem	CHAPTER 2	backstep analysis problem-clarification charts force-field analysis
Planning	CHAPTER 11	goal-attainment scaling
	CHAPTER 3	milestone charts Gantt charts
	CHAPTER 4	precedent diagrams time-scale networks
Deciding	CHAPTER 8	ordinal ranking weighted rating impact factoring
	CHAPTER 9	decision trees
Evaluating	CHAPTER 8	ordinal ranking weighted rating impact factoring
	CHAPTER 11	goal-attainment scaling
Describing Procedures and Directing People	CHAPTER 5	ADP flowcharts
	CHAPTER 6	decision logic tables
	CHAPTER 7	work flow charts document distribution chart process chart procedure chart
	CHAPTER 12	Warnier diagrams
Describing Entire Systems	CHAPTER 10	FAST diagrams
	CHAPTER 12	Warnier diagrams

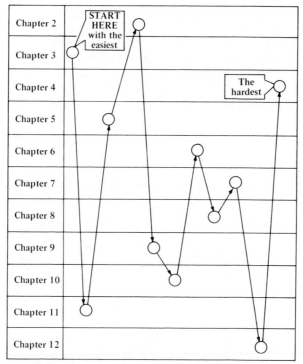

Follow the indicated path from Chapter 3 through the
progressively more challenging, chapters.

FIGURE 1.3: A guide for the timid.

relationship. For each of the types of problems listed the diagram displays the chapters which are pertinent and the tools that are presented in those chapters. The Warnier diagram facilitates both the organization and the description of the material.

Finally, Figure 1.3, "A Guide for the Timid," utilizes a variation of another tool, one called a workflow chart. It graphically describes a suggested sequence of reading the chapters. Here again, like the Warnier diagram, the essence of the workflow chart is probably best grasped without further explanation.

These and the other techniques presented have something in common: each is a technique that focuses on some kind of chart. Therefore, each chart is tangible, and is easily applied, both to analyze and to describe situations. The charts are not, however, the kind used to display numerical or statistical information. Rather, they are useful in the "management" of situations encountered daily.

The value of the tools

**In my experience, I have found that most people suffer from a po-
verty of models for solving problems. Most of us learn one or two
basic . . . solutions easily in our careers, and after that we proceed
to use the same models over and over to solve all problems, whether
they are appropriate or not.**

Ken Orr*

The common benefits of these tools are mentioned here once rather
than being cited in each chapter. All twenty tools are *tangible*—they
are graphical in nature, structured and accompanied by definable procedures that are easy to learn. By applying them and creating their associated chart, you inevitably develop an *understanding* of the situation confronted. The chart itself becomes *documentation* of the situation, problem, or procedure. The chart format is highly suitable for
analysis, that is, for spotting problem areas, potential improvements,
and alternatives. These, too, are describable, using the techniques
mentioned above. Next—and equally important to the others—the
chart formats are admirably suited to *communication* with all interested parties. The charts portray the facts clearly and easily and can be
understood and followed by nearly everyone.

Using the tools

A cook uses kitchen utensils to create an endless variety of dishes.
Once the cook knows the essential use of a meat cleaver or a stove, its
value is evident, and there is no need to list the entrees that can be prepared with them. So it is with our analytical tools, although some
generalizations are helpful.

Table 1.2 relates each tool to the general problem categories. Use
the table as a guide—but not blindly; real-world problems do not always fall into easily defined categories. Modify the basic models as
needed, and incorporate the unique aspects of your particular problem.

---

*Kenneth T. Orr, *Structured Systems Development*, New York: Yourdon Press, 1977, p.
61; reprinted with permission.

True, a particular tool is useful for a particular kind of problem. But most techniques are useful in several phases of the problem-solving process, or in what is often called the "scientific method":

1. Define the problem.
2. Collect data and analyze the facts.
3. List alternate solutions.
4. Select the best alternate.
5. Put it into effect (that is, implement the solution).
6. Evaluate the results.

For example, the process charts shown in Chapter 7 are used to describe the steps of a relatively simple process—something done by one person or on one piece of paper. The process chart can be used to collect data (describe the existing situation), generate alternatives (construct new approaches), and implement a chosen solution (for example, with everyone involved).

The executive [anyone?] who tries to solve problems by depending on abstract reasoning, experience, general information, memory, or a superficial survey of the problem situation is headed for ultimate disaster . . . . If you're lucky you may reach some correct solutions in this manner. But in the long run, you'll have a low batting average.

Dr. T. F. Stanton*

The cook finds a mixer and stove more expedient than a wood stick and a hot rock. But alas, having the tools does not make the cook a chef. Similarly, while you will find the analytic tools easy to master, you must add perspective, season with judgement, and garnish with human-relations skills. Without these, the finest implements and the best intentions may be unpalatable to those who believe they are being force-fed.

That's an overview of our subject. The strategy thus presented will guide your involvement. The following chapters, develop the specifics of each analytical tool.

---

*T. F. Stanton, "How to Simplify a Problem," in *Nation's Business*, U.S. Chamber of Commerce, June 1957.

2

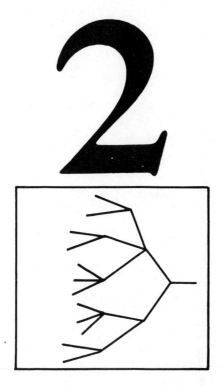

"Problem? I Don't See a Problem"

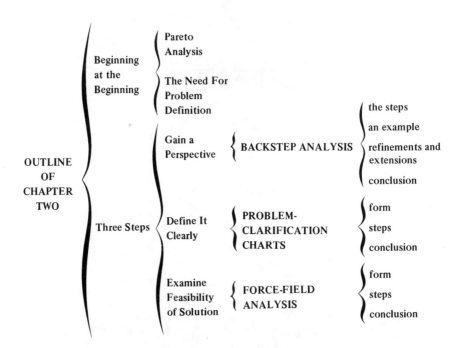

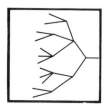

Beginning at the beginning

Recognizing a problem is frequently a subtle phenomenon. One reason is that a problem can be viewed in different ways. One might say that a problem is an obstacle to achieving a goal, another that it is a deviation from an ideal. Or one might take the opportunity to make an improvement and call it a problem, applying problem-solving approaches in making the improvement.

Regardless of viewpoint, problem selection is crucial. Why? Because our efforts are easily thwarted if we do not select problems properly. Figure 2.1 illustrates this. Begin at the far right and read left. Each branch to the left of the preceding branch is potentially a contributing cause of the problem on its right.

So our problem at this point is the proper selection and definition of a problem. Three analytical tools are useful here; but first let's add a useful technique, one that is not chart-based but which is still invaluable: Pareto analysis, based on the Pareto principle.

Pareto analysis

In any series of elements to be controlled, a selected, small fraction, in terms of the number of elements, always accounts for a large fraction in terms of effect.

Vilfredo Pareto (1848-1923)

The economist and sociologist Vilfredo Pareto observed a phenomenon that applies to nearly everything in modern life. His principle states that, for nearly any event or consequence, of all the contributing

15

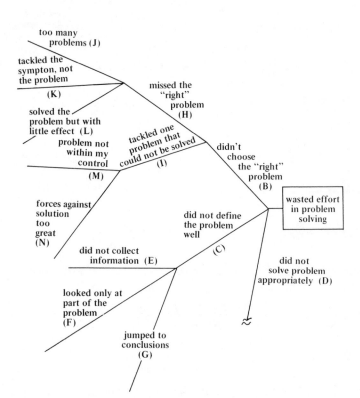

FIGURE 2.1

factors, only a small number will account for the bulk of the effect. This is often referred to as "the vital few versus the trivial many." Three examples will illustrate this principle.

1. Only a small percent of the thousands of inventory items in a department store account for 80% of the dollar sales. (Discount stores capitalized on this).
2. Less than 10% of the employees in an organization will account for most of the absenteeism.
3. A few percent of the kinds of illnesses are the cause of admission for the great majority of hospital patients.

The examples are inexhaustible; the point is that the principal can be applied to nearly everything. Therefore, maximize your efforts by applying the Pareto principle in focusing your energies. How do we do this? Two general examples will illustrate.

Suppose you listed, without evaluation, the problems you see around you. Now order them, beginning with the ones causing the greatest difficulty, that is, those with those having the greatest effect, and continuing down to the minor problems. At the top of the list would be the "significant few," and below would be the "trivial many." The greatest results for a given amount of effort come from tackling the significant few.

Similarly, if you zero in on an area to improve, and try to solve it, you should first "Pareto-ize" the factors causing or influencing the problem. You may find a particular factor more worthy of concentration than any of the others. Can you see how this approach will help you avoid the traps represented by branches B, H, J, and L of Figure 2.1?

The need for problem definition

Many business problems are made worse by a need to solve the problems before they have been correctly diagnosed. Would it not be useful then to better identify the problems?

J. D. Warnier*

Many other traps remain as branches of Figure 2.1, which we dare not ignore. Imagine a train engineer approaching a switching station that governs a fork of multiple tracks. Oblivious to the position of the switch, the engineer is thus fated to rush forward onto a track, not knowing whether it is to the correct track. Each of us has known people who act similarly in their personal affairs or in their work. "To avoid doing it over, do it right the first time!" Three quickly grasped tools follow, which will help the reader accomplish this.

Three steps

Three successive steps guide you to correctly defining the current problem, each step using its own tool. They are:

1. Gain a perspective—using Backstep Analysis
2. Define it clearly—using Problem Clarification Charts
3. Examine feasibility of solution—using Force Field Analysis

The remainder of this chapter is devoted to explaining these tools.

---

*Kenneth T. Orr, *Structured Systems Development*, New York: Yourdon Press, 1977; reprinted with permission.

Backstep analysis

We would be deceiving ourselves by treating the symptoms of a problem and not the problem itself. A five-year old boy, covered with hives, was taken to a physician for treatment. The astute doctor, prior to dispensing lotions, inquired whether the boy had suffered stress of any kind. He had indeed; a week before the boy witnessed the hit-and-run, and subsequent death, of his beloved dog. The doctor's prescription? "Buy the boy another dog." Once done, the problem was solved.

Seldom are situations so straightforward as to involve only a single problem and its symptoms.

Usually the causes of the problem are themselves problems with multiple causes. To solve these subproblems, look to the simple, yet powerful, process called backstep analysis.

Figure 2.1 is the diagram that results from backstep analysis. The problem—"wasted effort in problem solving"—is at the right. Toward the left are progressively underlying causes and/or problems that contribute to the wasted effort. The diagram is used to put the issue in perspective.

The steps

Create a Backstep diagram by performing these steps:

(1) Taking a blank sheet of paper, draw a box in the middle of the right-hand side. Using as few words as possible, write within the box the main problem as you see it. From this point on, we will be working right to left.

(2) To the left of the problem box—and from it—draw as many radiating lines as you believe are the principal causes of the problem. Again, label each one, using as few words as possible.

(3) For each cause, continue the process, working right to left, until a logical stopping point becomes clear. This process is called backstep analysis because, at each step, we "step back" and analyze the underlying cause or causes of the problem.

(4) When you have completed the diagram, zero in on the portion that falls within your control or influence. Screen this portion further by Pareto-izing, to select the factors significant enough to warrant effort.

This then becomes your problem. You may do more by reducing in half the biggest cause than you could by eliminating all the other causes.

An example

A manager, somewhat unfairly has just vented to a nearby clerk, frustrations over "late receipt of mailed packages" by the firm's clients. The clerk, attempting to clarify why this occurs, commences a Backstep Analysis.

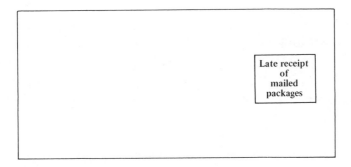

FIGURE 2.2

Potential contributing causes of the problem come to mind. (There is no need at this point to discern which are actual causes and which are potential causes; that can be done at a later time). Two are immediately obvious and so labeled as shown.

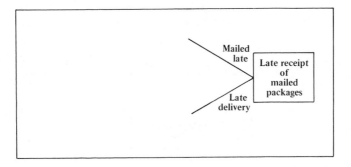

FIGURE 2.3

Each of these may be described as arising for still other reasons. Those causes are added to the diagram in their logical position.

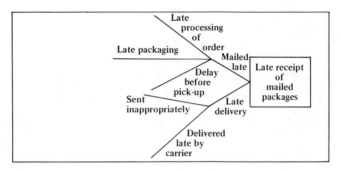

FIGURE 2.4

The process is continued as long as needed. Our clerk concludes that the below Backstep Diagram in Figure 2.5 is sufficient to organize an investigation of the facts.

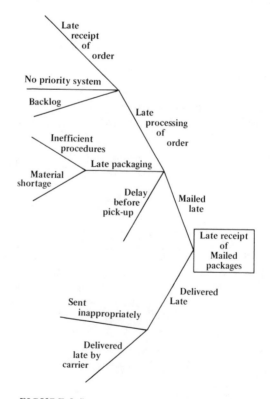

FIGURE 2.5

Probably the lowest set of branches are outside the clerk's domain of influence; the "problem" would then be localized on one of the upper branches.

Refinements and extensions

To our basic Backstep Diagram, several observations are pertinent.

1. If typing and a neat preparation of the diagram is a concern, this may be facilitated by changing the format slightly.

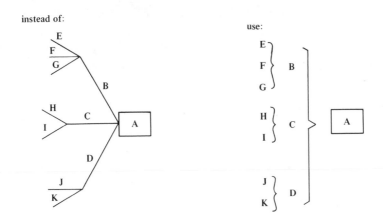

FIGURE 2.6

2. The mere appearance of the diagram can indicate difficulties in the analysis. Below are three examples.

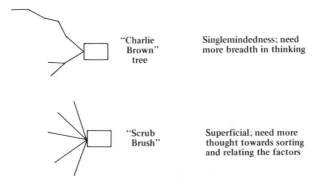

FIGURE 2.7: Diagnosing backstep diagrams (continued).

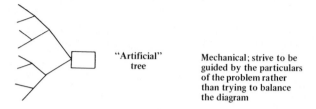

"Artificial"
tree

Mechanical; strive to be
guided by the particulars
of the problem rather
than trying to balance
the diagram

FIGURE 2.7: Diagnosing backstep diagrams (continued).

3. (Cause-Effect diagrams*): What we've done so far is a Backstep Diagram for problem definition only. Displaying the resulting effects or consequences is also possible. When this is done we develop a double-sided tree with the given problem in the middle. The causes are developed to the left as done above. The tree form grows to the right with the primary effects first and next the secondary effects.

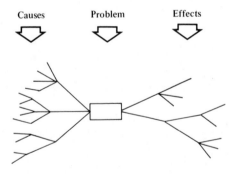

Causes   Problem   Effects

*FIGURE 2.8: Cause-effect diagrams.**

Backstep analysis is used to gain a perspective of the many levels that are associated with most problems. Invaluable as it is, such analysis alone will not enable us to avoid the traps shown in Figure 2.1. Two additional tools round out our repertoire of problem-defining techniques—problem clarification charts and force field analysis. To repeat, use all three in sequence.

*Cause-effect diagrams are widely acclaimed in Japan, where they are known as "Tokusei-Yoin Hyo" or "Ishikawa diagrams," after their inventor, Kaora Ishikawa of Tokyo University.

Problem clarification charts

Almost any problem can be solved that can be adequately stated.

–from an IBM film entitled "The Glossary."

In tackling problems, be aggressive but not impetuous. Assess before you pounce. Study your challenge before you act, lest you fail or disappoint all who assist you. State your problem adequately by first assessing its scope. This is where problem clarification charts come in.

Steps

Figure 2.9 illustrates such a chart. The format—or even the chart itself—is relatively unimportant; it merely aids what *is* important: making the effort to clarify the problem.

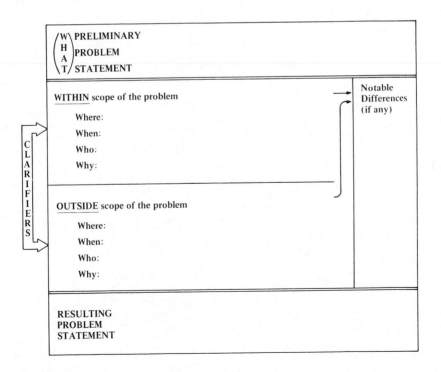

FIGURE 2.9: Problem clarification chart

Follow these steps in clarifying the problem:

1. Begin with a preliminary statement of your problem.

2. Gather information about the problem; seek to define its boundaries. What is *within* the scope of the problem? What is *outside* its scope? Separate these viewpoints and your conclusions, using the chart to prompt your inquiry, and record your findings. Then you may be able to discern some notable differences. For example, knowing when the problem occurs and does not occur may be significant, leading to a clearer understanding of the true problem.

> *I keep six honest serving men (they taught me all I knew). Their names are What and Why and When and How and Where and Who.*
>
> Rudyard Kipling

Key words can be used to prod the investigation, words that have ably served Rudyard Kipling, Sherlock Holmes, and many other investigators. Let them serve you. They are:

WHAT is the concern? —the magnitude? —the importance?

WHERE did or does it occur (geographically, organizationally, or sequentially)?

WHEN did or does it occur? Was it observed?

WHO was or was not affected by it? Who observed it? Who caused it?

WHY did or does it occur?

It is not necessary to enter facts in each cell, but you should ask each question above. (If you have done a backstep analysis, you may already have information under *why*.)

3. When you have gathered information, redefine the problem in light of the information.

Conclusion

Discipline yourself to do this analysis. The rewards will be a higher rate of success and less wasted effort. You will frequently discover that the concluding problem statement differs substantially from the initial premise. For example, a Navy installation appeared to have a flagrant sick leave-abuse problem. A problem-clarification analysis performed to delineate the problem yielded some surprising results. Sick leave was indeed high but not through abuse. The problem was located in a paint plant, which during cold months was closed to keep it warm. The concluding problem statement addressed the lack of proper ventilation equipment, not the abuse of sick leave!

The traps in Figure 2.1 remain despite our use of both backstep analysis and problem clarification charts. One, in particular, stands out: branch N, "forces against solution too great." To aid us here, force field analysis is used.

Force-field analysis

So you have chosen a significant problem, analyzed the causes, and defined it clearly. Should you now jump into the fun part—namely, solving the problem? A force-field analysis, which is quickly done, is used to assess the feasibility of solving the problem. Here's how. Figure 2.10 shows the general form of the technique.

Steps

Perform force-field analysis, using the form in Figure 2.10 and following these steps:

1. Begin with a problem statement and reword it, making it a positive statement of action or goal to be achieved. Enter the statement on the worksheet in the space marked *goal*.

2. To the left of the middle line, list all *favoring* forces, that is, the factors that promote achievement of the goal. Identify briefly each force, placing the identification above the arrow indicated.

3. Similarly, list to the right of the middle line the *inhibiting* forces, that is, those hampering successful achievement of the goal.

4. Assess the relative strength of each factor listed, giving both those that favor achievement of the goal and those that inhibit it. Indicate their importance by the length of the arrow you draw under each factor. The longer the arrow, the stronger the force.

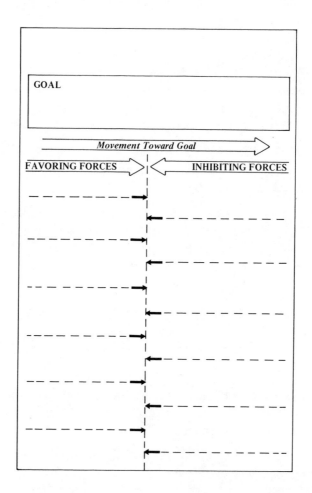

GOAL

Movement Toward Goal

FAVORING FORCES   INHIBITING FORCES

FIGURE 2.10: *Force-field analysis worksheet*

Now you have a graphical assessment of the feasibility of solving a problem. Equally valuable is the knowledge of what must be overcome and what favors a successful solution.

CONCLUSION

This chapter presents the concepts of Pareto Analysis, Backstep Analysis, Problem Clarification Charting, and Force Field Analysis. They assist in the selection, definition and assessment of your "problem". As to problem solution, Chapter One outlines an approach, the scientific method (see page 11). The chapters which follow offer specific techniques which, depending on your kind of problem, will help solve it.

3

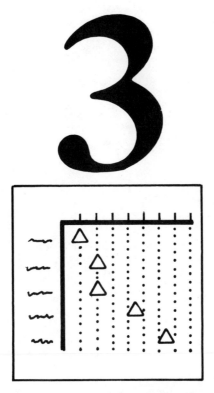

"You Want It When?"

OUTLINE
OF
CHAPTER
THREE
{

Choosing
Between
Failure and
Success

Two
Techniques
{

MILESTONE
CHARTS
{
purpose
form
steps

GANTT
CHARTS
{
form
to track progress
steps

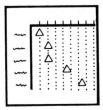

Choosing between failure and success

You have the responsibility for a project. It may be moving to larger facilities, reorganizing an entire office, or coordinating the replacement of old equipment. Whatever it is, it's an important, nontrivial effort involving a number of tasks, all of which must be done successfully if the project is to succeed. Considerable time is involved, as well as, perhaps, the assistance or cooperation of other people. The approach to this responsibility is crucial.

Inadvertently, you could precipitate a failure by following a *recipe for disaster.*

1. Assume that you can proceed unilaterally.

2. Wait two weeks to begin.

3. Save time by not planning.

4. Start the easiest task first.

5. Begin a second task.

6. Recruit help.

7. Initiate a third task.

8. Accelerate the second task.

9. Involve more people.

10. Rationalize delays.

11. Try to kill the project.

12. Adopt a policy of nonintervention.

13. Panic.

14. Misplace blame.

15. Disavow association.

16. Transfer to another project.

Unfortunately, this is a recipe that is more realistic than fictitious. Assuming this is not what you want to do, how can you approach your project constructively? Consider using a milestone chart or a Gantt chart. As an illustration, consider a fairly simple project, the preparation and distribution of announcements for a symposium. This will be our example throughout this chapter.

Milestone charts

A milestone chart displays the planned, significant events in the progress of a project. Approval points and target-completion dates for major tasks are typical. In the example given, the chart might appear as shown in Figure 3.1.

Milestones—that is, due dates for significant events—are established in advance—from project commencement to project completion. All interested parties now have a visual plan of what must be accomplished and when it must be done.

Form

Figure 3.2 represents the components of a milestone chart. A time scale appears across the top of the chart, and the activities and events are listed in a column to the left, in a downward, chronological sequence. This causes the milestones to fall in a general pattern of upper left to lower right. The milestones themselves are usually represented by a hollow figure, such as a triangle. Thus project progress can be displayed by shading in the milestones—when, in fact, that milestone has been achieved.

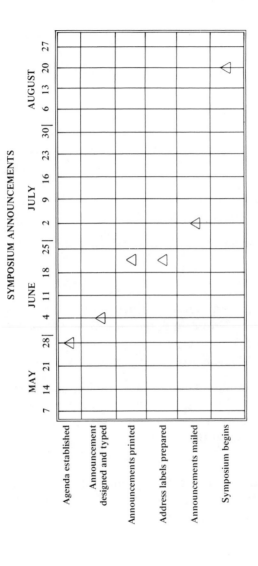

FIGURE 3.1: Milestone chart.

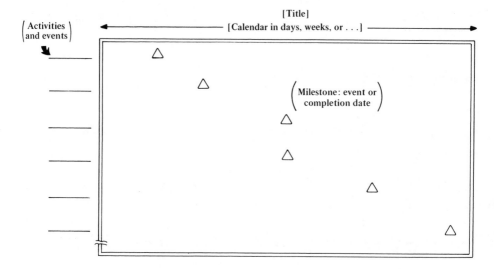

FIGURE 3.2: General form of a milestone chart.

Steps

Only three steps are required to construct a milestone chart:

1. Determine the significant activities and events essential to project achievement. To do this, people usually prefer to begin at the starting point of the project and work forward to completion.

2. Determine the time required for completion of each activity and event. Here, most prefer to begin with an established project completion date, such as the end point, and work backward, fixing the completion time of the other points.

3. Make a milestone chart. Provide enough room for the calendar to span the entire chart—from the time of the start of the project to the end of the project. List activities and events in a downward sequence by milestone date.

Gantt charts

Our milestone chart ensures that we do not follow a *"recipe for disaster."* However, a simple effort converts the Milestone Chart to a Gantt chart—which is substantially better for planning and controlling a project. On this chart, starting times and activity durations supplement completion times. For our sample project, a Gantt chart such as that shown in Figure 3.3 is used.

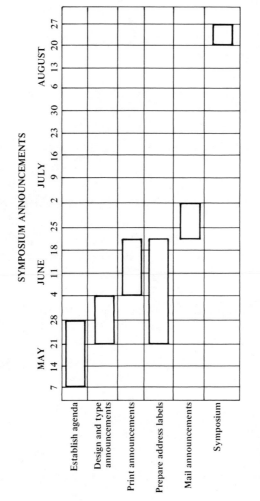

FIGURE 3.3: Gantt chart for symposium announcements

The chart displays useful information such as the expected duration of each activity, and therefore, gives an indication of the latest time at which each activity should begin, thus avoiding delaying its completion time.

Form

Gantt charts use a form similar to that of milestone charts. In a Gantt chart, though, the milestone symbol is replaced by a horizontal rectangle, with the right end of the rectangle representing the target termination time. The horizontal length signifies the duration of the activity. Thus the left end suggests a latest starting time for the activity. Draft the Gantt chart, using hollow rectangles (the reason for doing this is explained next).

Using the Gantt chart as a progress tracking tool

Useful as a planning tool, the Gantt chart serves equally well as a control for tracking progress. As any given activity is partially completed, shade in its rectangle on the left. If any activity is 25 percent complete as of today, shade in the leftmost quarter of the rectangle. (Refer to Figure 3.4 for the sample project, "Symposium Announcements".)

Assume that today's date is May 25, as represented by the dashed vertical line in Figure 3.4. Assessed progress on each activity is indicated by proportionate shading of that activity's rectangle. One immediately observes that, as of today, "established agenda" is on schedule, "design and type announcement" is behind, and "prepare address labels" is ahead of schedule.

Steps

The steps associated with Gantt charting are:

A. Create the chart for planning purposes by:

   1. Determining the activities essential to project achievement.

   2. Determining, for each activity, both a target-completion date and its expected duration.

   3. Drafting the chart, listing activities in chronological sequence by their ending target dates. Represent each with a rectangle appropriately placed, with a horizontal length appropriate to its expected duration.

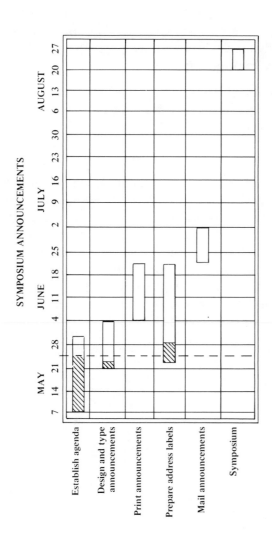

FIGURE 3.4: Gantt chart used for tracking progress

B. Use the chart to track progress:

1. For each activity, do the following on a regular basis: as progress is made in the activity, assess an approximate percentage of progress toward completion of the activity. Represent this progress by a proportionate shading of the activity's rectangle, beginning from the left.

2. Use a movable, vertical line to represent the current date. (Discrepancies between the actual and the expected progress will be manifest.)

CONCLUSION

The let's-start-out-and-see-if-we-make-it approach can sink the person responsible for a project. The wise project manager, therefore, transforms a large project into smaller, more manageable segments by establishing when the subparts must be finished and how long each is expected to take. Structure this against a calendar, and presto, you have a planning *and* progress-tracking tool. Milestone and Gantt charts are indeed beneficial. If you think the Gantt chart is an improvement over the milestone chart, read on; Chapter 4 presents some techniques by comparison with that pales Gantt charting.

4

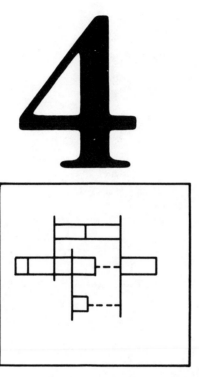

"It Can't Be Done by Then!"

OUTLINE
OF
CHAPTER
FOUR

Getting Started
{
the tools {
PRECEDENT DIAGRAM
TIME-SCALE NETWORK
}
their value
structure of
this chapter
}

Basic
Elements
{
activities
network
time
critical path
}

Sample
Project

Level I:
Activities
{
value
preview
steps
our example
}

Level II:
Timing
{
value
calculating times
critical path
slack times
TIME-SCALE NETWORKS
}
{
an example
value
steps
our example
project
}

Sample
Project

Level III:
Resources
{
value
an example
steps
our example project
}

Footnotes
{
value
PERT/CPM
a reminder
}

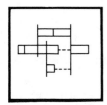

Getting started

Let us define a project as a significant undertaking that involves a number of tasks and that has a recognizable completion, or target, date with definite results. To illustrate, "providing physical exams to 50 people by 19 September" is a project. "Promoting improved health," however, is an ongoing program, not a project.

The tools and their value

Chapter 3 discusses two tools (the milestone chart and the Gantt chart) used to help ensure the successful completion of a project. In recent years these concepts have evolved, yielding two even more useful tools, precedent diagrams and time-scale charts. (You may have heard of the related forms, PERT and CPM.)

Precedent diagrams and time-scale charts, the subject of this chapter, permit one to visualize the following:

–all essential activities
–the relationship of activities
–the duration and timing of each activity
–critical activities, that is, those which, if delayed, can delay completion of the project
–scheduling approaches in order to level out the workload

Thus, from the beginning, one has some degree of control over a project. A more specific discussion of the value of these activities and approaches occurs at selected points in this chapter and at its conclusion.

*He who is dumb enough to get behind is probably not smart enough
to catch up.*

A corollary of Wynne's Law.

Structure of chapter

Knowing the chapter's structure will help you maintain your perspective of the topic. It takes the following form. First, the four basic elements of the two tools are enumerated. Second, a sample problem (or project) is presented, which, in this chapter, serves the purpose of illustration. Third, explanations are given.

These tools have many features and each reader will have different needs. Someone, for instance, may desire only the basic features, with thus, the remainder being unimportant "bells and whistles"; whereas others may require the tools' full power. The topic is divided into three levels to facilitate extracting only that which is needed.

Level 1 focuses on the *activities* of a project—what they are, their order, and their relationship. Given this, *Level 2* focuses on the *timing* of the activities, providing information on their duration and their start and stop times. This level also provides insight into which activities are crucial in their timing and which can be "slipped," and by how long. When this has been established, *Level 3* focuses on the *resources* needed to complete this project. The level permits scheduling activities to reflect and optimize the resources available (usually people).

The chapter concludes with some hints about the value of the tools discussed, and ends with a few comments.

Basic elements

The four basic elements are the *activities*, or *tasks*; the *network*; the *time*; and the *critical path*. The activities, or tasks, are the specific, identifiable units of effort that must occur in accomplishment of the project. No general rule is possible as to the magnitude of effort that should be considered. Such a rule is situation-specific. The example given may help put this in perspective.

The network is the diagrammatic sequence of activities and their relationship to each other. It is our chart.

When the time, or expected duration of each activity, is added to the network, a metamorphosis occurs. A schedule is created that gives duration, starting times, slippage possibilities, and so forth.

Once time is portrayed, a critical path becomes evident. This path is the sequence of crucial activities that have something in common. If the completion of any activity is delayed, the entire project will be delayed.

A sample project

The following scenario outlines a project that will serve as an illustration for the remainder of this chapter. (It is a more realistic expansion of the symposium-announcement example given in Chapter 3.) Suppose you are responsible for planning and preparing a major symposium. You are told that the symposium is to begin forty-five working days from now and that the largest possible audience is desired. Although it is not specifically stated, the implied list of your concerns includes an agenda, the speakers, announcements, space, catering, and conference materials. Somewhat awed by all this, you give the symposium the name "Operation Aaagh!". Let us see how precedent diagrams and time-scale charting can help you avoid panic and control the situation.

Level 1: activities

At Level 1, we introduce the precedent diagram. It facilitates understanding the activities that are involved, their sequence and relationships. By relationships, we mean the characteristics of dependence and independence among the activities. Knowing which activities can begin *only after* others are completed is important. The precedent chart will help you do this.

To permit you to see where you are headed, the concluding precedent diagram (at this level, Level 1) for "Operation Aaagh!" is shown in Figure 4.1. (At this point, ignore the letter assignments for each activity.)

Steps

Now let's see how the diagram is created.

First, identify the activities, or tasks, that are involved, and their relationship. Second, construct the chart. Specifically, perform the following steps:

1. *List activities*. List all the significant activities involved in accomplishing the project. Note that the order is not important at this

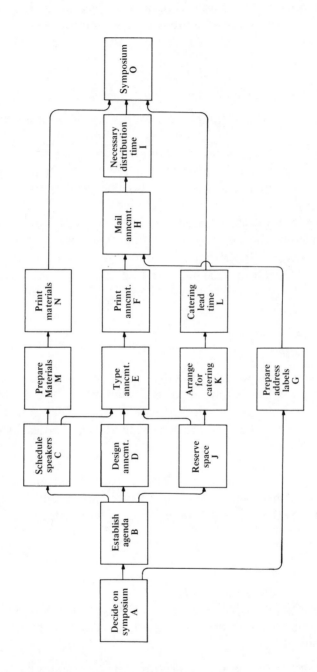

FIGURE 4.1: Precedent diagram for symposium project

point. Either of two approaches can be used: *brainstorming*—that is, not concerning yourself with order, but listing all the approaches that occur to you as quickly as they occur, or *systematically* looking at the project from the beginning, working forward through the activities.

2. *Determine sequence.* For each activity listed, determine: (a) what other activities must be completed immediately before the one in question can begin, and (b) what other activities cannot begin until it is completed.

3. *Construct the chart.* Draft the precedent diagram, using this information and following the charting conventions described later.

Our example thus begins. One popular method is to write each project activity on a seperate piece of paper. Precision is not essential at this point; you will certainly add, delete, or change some of the activities as you go along. Move each one around, attempting to place the activity in its proper position, relative to all the others. When you're finished, copy the results in finished form. To visualize this, refer to Figure 4.1 while imagining each activity being written on movable pieces of paper. Essentially unstructured, the above method is not amendable to precise description; hence, an *alternative* approach is described. First, list the activities that appear to be major ones. Begin with the decision to hold the symposium, and end with the actual conference. Table 4.1 reveals thirteen tasks that fall between these two.

Note that both the decision to hold the symposium and the symposium itself are listed intentionally. Further, two items—(I) necessary distribution time, and (L) catering lead time—are tasks that do not actually have to be performed. Although they aren't tasks, these are essential timings that must be considered, and therefore, are included.

Next, fill in the column labeled "immediately preceded by" in Table 4.1. Examples? Whereas nothing precedes A (decide on symposium), it is obvious that B (establish agenda) must be preceded immediately by the decision. Consider item E (type announcements). This activity can be done only after we have all the information necessary and after we have determined the announcement layout. Thus, three tasks must preceed the typing: C (schedule speakers); D (design announcements); and J (reserve space). Similarly, all activities are considered, and Table 4.2 is the result. (Review it to assure comprehension.)

TABLE 4.1: Activity List for Symposium Project.

Task	Description	Immediately preceded by	Immediately followed by
A	Decide on symposium		
B	Establish agenda		
C	Schedule speakers		
D	Design announcements		
E	Type announcements		
F	Print announcements		
G	Prepare address labels		
H	Mail announcements		
I	Necessary distribution time		
J	Reserve space		
K	Arrange for catering		
L	Catering lead time		
M	Prepare materials		
N	Print materials		
O	Symposium		

Now fill in the column labeled "immediately followed by." The result is shown in Table 4.2. You have now established the sequence and relationship of the activities.

Conventions

At this point we need to know the conventions of the precedent diagrams. They are:

Each box represents a distinct task or activity.

Time flow is left to right.

The project begins from only one box, and all paths end at one box; all activities are placed in their logical sequence.

No activity can begin until all activities leading to a particular activity are complete.

Lines may be crossed, but their meaning must be clear.

TABLE 4.2: *Activity List after Consideration.*

Task	Description	Immediately preceded by	Immediately followed by
A	Decide on symposium	—	B,G
B	Establish agenda	A	C,D,J
C	Schedule speakers	B	E,M
D	Design announcements	B	E
E	Type announcements	C,D,J	F
F	Print announcements	E	H
G	Prepare address labels	A	H
H	Mail announcements	F,G	I
I	Necessary distribution time	H	O
J	Reserve space	B	E,K
K	Arrange for catering	J	L
L	Catering lead time	K	O
M	Prepare materials	C	N
N	Print materials	M	O
O	Symposium	N,I,L	—

All connectors *from* an activity emanate from the righthand vertical line of the box; all connectors *to* an activity terminate at the lefthand vertical line of the box. Arrowheads on the connectors are used to avoid confusion. These conventions are illustrated in Figure 4.2.

Avoid making two common errors: the dangle activity and the loop activity. A dangled activity is one that lacks either a preceding or a subsequent activity, and therefore is in error. (Two exceptions are the first activity and the last activity.) A loop is a series of activities that flow in a circular direction.

Summary

Turn back to Figure 4.1 and reexamine the logic of the precedent diagram. It tells us what has to be done and in what sequence. You can now begin to grasp what the symposium project entails. Yet, vital information is lacking that you need to successfully meet your project responsibilities. Turn to the considerations of Level II, discussed next.

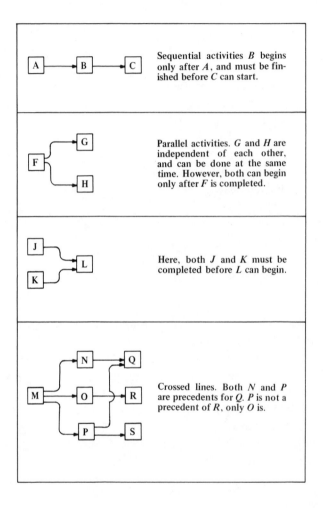

FIGURE 4.2: *Understanding precedent diagrams*

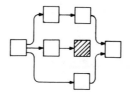

The "Dangle"

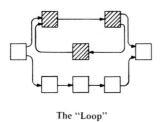

The "Loop"

FIGURE 4.3: Two common errors

Level II: timing

At the Level II stage we incorporate considerations of time. Essentially, we estimate the duration required for each activity, then use that estimate to draw several useful conclusions.

By incorporating time considerations, we gain valuable insight into:

—the minimum time for completing the project

—the activities that fall on the critical path

—the activities with slack time available; that is, those that may be delayed

—the earliest and the latest starting (and finishing) times for each activity

Because all this is available graphically, it can be communicated readily.

Preview

Again, let us see where the technique leads. The concluding time-scale chart of what our problem will be is shown in Figure 4.4.

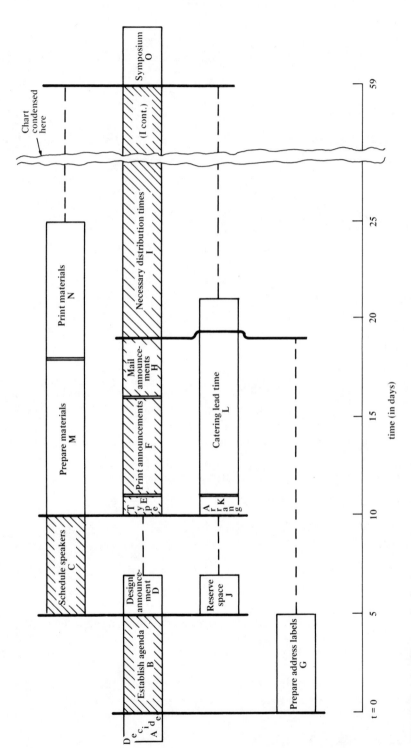

FIGURE 4.4: Time-scale chart

The value of the chart is apparent. For one thing, the critical path is shown. Correlate the critical path to the time scale at the bottom, to determine the length of the project. Now compare the total time needed with the problem as given. You should discover a contradiction: the diagram shows the project as consuming fifty-nine days, whereas the original instructions specify forty-five. This is one reason why you benefit by executing a network diagram of the project *at the start.* Other advantages are discussed later. The task at hand is to show the development of this chart.

Steps

The steps involved in creating the Level II Precedent diagram are:

1. Estimate the duration of the activities.

2. Calculate the *earliest* start time and the finish time for each activity.

3. Identify the critical path.

4. (*optional*) Calculate the *latest* start time and the finish time for each activity.

Our sample project will serve as an illustration as each step is elaborated in detail.

1. Estimate activity durations.

For each task, you must estimate a reasonable (not optimistic or pessimistic, but reasonable) expected time for performing the task. If other people are involved in the tasks, ask them for an estimate. (You should get others involved as early as possible, and this is one way to do it.) The earlier precedent diagram is modified to include the expected duration for each activity (see Fig. 4.5).

2. Calculate the earliest start times.

Here, we need two definitions:

Earliest finish (EF)

is the earliest time we can reasonably expect to finish a task. Assume we know the earliest time a task can be started is $t = 7$ and the expected duration of the task to be 5 units of time. Then the earliest the task will be completed is $t = 12$, or time equals earliest start plus duration.

52

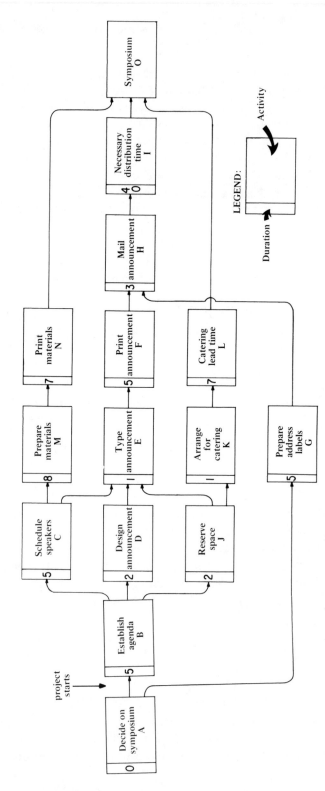

FIGURE 4.5: Symposium precedent diagram with durations

Earliest start (ES)

is the earliest time at which an activity can begin. This time is dictated by the activities immediately preceding the given activity. The rule here is: the earliest start for a given activity will be the latest finish time of all the activities immediately preceding it. By way of illustrating the logic of this rule, refer to Figure 4.6. All three activities, N, I, and L must be completed before activity O can begin. The earliest finish times of N, I, *and* L are as shown. Therefore, O must wait to commence until $t = 59$, the latest of these three finish times.

The principles used in calculating the earliest start times can be stated as follows:

The start time for the first activity is $t = 0$.

The start time for the immediately succeeding activities will be the time at which the first activity is finished.

For all remaining activities, the earliest time that each can start is dictated by the activities immediately preceding it. Because all preceding activities must first be completed, the earliest an activity can start is the latest of the earliest finish times of all immediately preceding activities.

Figure 4.7 is a precedent diagram for the symposium, showing the earliest start and finish times for all activities.

3. Identify the critical path.

The critical path is outlined in Figure 4.7 by heavy flow lines. Identify the critical path by working from right to left, tracing the path that al-

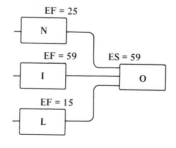

FIGURE 4.6

54

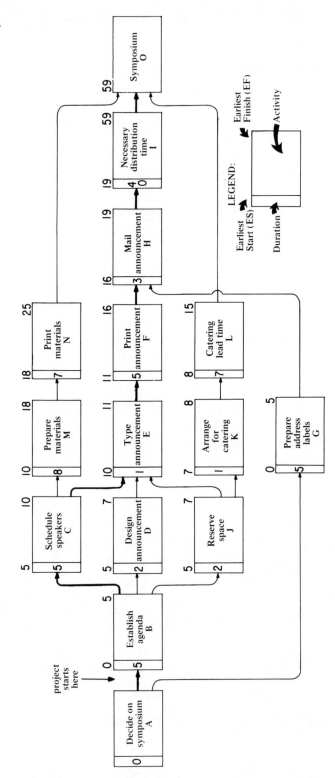

FIGURE 4.7: Symposium diagram with earlist start and finish times

ways gives the latest earliest finish time. Review Figure 4.7 until this is clear. Any delay in activities B, C, E, F, H, or I is critical to the project.

For our symposium project, we now see that, if we start on time and if we accomplish each step without delay, 59 days are needed. Recall, however, that you were directed to have the symposium begin in 45 days. The precedent diagram alerts you early to this discrepancy. Your reaction? Negotiate for (a) delay of the symposium to 59 days, (b) recognition that less than 40 days for distribution of the announcement will probably result in fewer attendees, or (c) additional resources to shorten the duration of critical activities.

4. Calculate the latest start and finish times for each activity. *

You calculated the *earliest* time for each activity; you may also calculate the *latest* start time for each activity. The reason for doing this is to calculate the "slack". The difference between the earliest start time and the latest start time gives you the slack. Slack is the amount of time available for delaying an activity. (Of course, critical activities have no slack.) Slack time is flexibility. One calculates latest start and stop times (to get slack) to determine the flexibility available.

Because this step is optional, it is outlined briefly here. In contrast to determining earliest times, work backward to calculate latest times; that is, begin with the final activity and work back to the first. Either construct a table for your calculations or add them to your chart. Figure 4.8 shows the process, using a chart.

The rules may be stated as follows:

Work backward, beginning at the terminal activity.

The earliest start time for the terminal activity becomes the latest finish time for each activity immediately preceding.

The latest start time for an activity equals the latest finish time minus the duration: $LS = LF - D$.

When a given activity has multiple, succeeding activities (to its right), use this as a guide. Look at the latest start times of these succeeding activities. Pick out the earliest of the latest start times. Use as the latest finish time for a given activity, the earliest latest-start of all the succeeding activities (to the right of the given activity.)

Calculate slack time thus: $S = LF - EF$, or $S = LS - ES$.

*Skip this step in your first reading, returning to it later only if you wish.

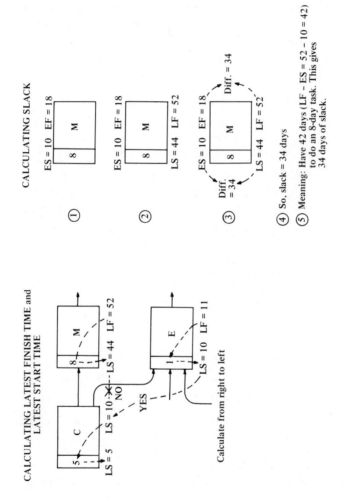

FIGURE 4.8: *Calculating latest times and slack*

Time-scale charts

The time-scale chart is a variant of the precedent diagram. Figure 4.9 shows both formats for a seven-activity situation. Compare them.

Note what the two formats have in common. Both display the activities, their duration, their relationship, and critical path. An important difference between them is the nature of the individual activities. The precedent diagram displays the activities uniformly, whereas the time-scale chart elongates the box that represents an activity in proportion to its duration.

A time-scale chart depicts all that a precedent diagram does, but additionally, correlates the tasks to a time scale. This reveals several things. Relative durations and critical path activities become more obvious, and slack time (both where and how much) is presented graphically. Look at Figure 4.9 again.

Equally important, as we shall see in Level III, is the property of sliding noncritical activities within the slack zone. For example, in Figure 4.9, imagine moving activity V in different positions along its slack band between tasks T and Y. You can thus visualize the flexibility available in the project—something that is not apparent in the precedent diagram.

Steps

How is a time-scale chart constructed? Construction is easy, since you've got half the work done with your precedent diagram. In general, follow these steps:

1. Make a precedent diagram
   (a) List all activities.
   (b) Determine sequences and relationships.
   (c) Draw the precedent diagram
   (d) Estimate durations.

2. Convert the precedent diagram to a time-scale chart
   (a) Lay out a time line.
   (b) Draw each activity with its length proportionate to its duration. As a matter of convention, place each activity at its earliest starting point, that is, as far left as possible.
   (c) Use vertical bars to denote dependencies between activities on different lines.
   (d) Denote slack by a dotted, horizontal line.
   (e) Highlight activities along the critical path.

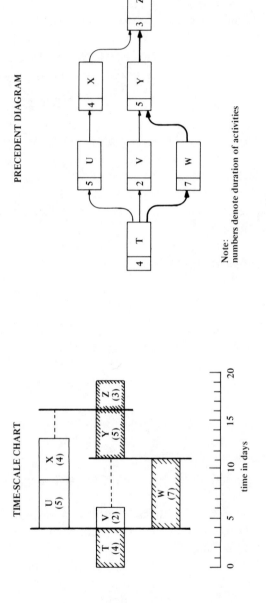

FIGURE 4.9: Compare chart types

Now refer to Figure 4.4, in which the Level II representation of the project is previewed. The time-scale chart graphically shows that the person dictating project completion in 45 days cannot have it by then. The chart services as a firm foundation for your assertions, as well as the basis for negotiations for change.

You may become enamored of time-scale charts. They graphically portray what you'd like others to understand and appreciate. They forcibly instill the need for responsiveness in people at the beginning of a project, that period when people tend to become complacent. In general, converting your precedent diagram to a time-scale chart is well worth the extra effort.

Level III: resources

Levels I and II have brought us this far. You have diagrammed the project and thus know the durations and relationship of all the activities as well as the timing of the overall project. But so far, nothing has addressed the resources—usually people—needed for the project. Level III considers resources and adjustment of the project schedule. This, in turn, enhances the probability of completing the project. Successfully: on time, by happy, rather than disgruntled people.

An Example

To illustrate what is at issue here, look at the same time-scale chart that we studied above. How do we display the fact that various people are involved in different activities? One popular technique uses color coding of activities to depict respective responsibilities.

Now focus on this thought: the same chart (Fig. 4.10) is annotated to show the number of people needed to work each day on the various tasks. How many people are needed each day of the project? What is the distribution of labor?

By now you should have added up, for any given day, the people needed on each task for all the tasks performed that day. Compare this total with Figure 4.11. Figure 4.12, however, displays a much improved situation. A more uniform, even distribution of labor is achieved simply by shifting activities U and X along their slack lines.

Notice the improvement from Figure 4.11 to Figure 4.12. The shifting of activities U and X evened out the workload dramatically. The project originally required as many as seven people; now no more than five are needed.

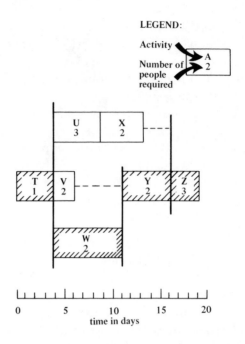

*FIGURE 4.10: Time-scale chart showing
people need by activity*

Levels I and II produced a time-scale chart giving activities, critical path, and slack time. Now, in Level III, we consider scheduling the flexible activities in light of the resources available for these activities. The time-scale chart allows us to adjust activities along their slack lines. We do this to level out the workload—the demands on our resources (usually people).

Steps

Enumerating the steps in projecting resource scheduling is straightforward; doing them draws on one's concentration and skills. Simply stated, the steps are:

1. Draft a time-scale chart.

2. Determine the resources needed—for example, people and equipment.

3. Level resources by shifting noncritical activities along their slack lines.

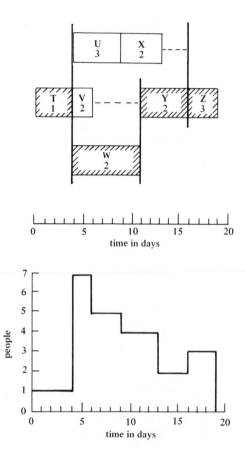

FIGURE 4.11

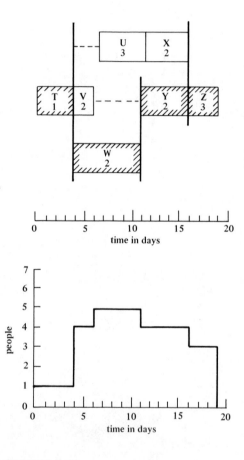

FIGURE 4.12

4. Level further by negotiating trade-offs in cost and time. If you accept a higher cost, you can secure additional resources, such as hiring temporaries. Less resources are needed if more time is granted for spreading out the resources currently available. Many more trade-offs may occur to the imaginative person faced with the responsibility for a project.

Suppose you are responsible for the symposium project, Presumably, some activities will be done by someone else, for example, printing announcements and materials. Assume that all other activities are to be done by you alone. Look at Figure 4.4 again, remembering that the chart was condensed at the right so it would fit on the page. If you tackled the project as shown, on some days you will be frantic, whereas on others, you will be utterly bored. How do you adjust activities so as to balance the workload confronting you? See Figure 4.4 to arrive at what you felt would be the best solution.

SUMMARY

Most people have, at one time or another, tackled a project without these tools and without a plan. Have you suppressed the memory of muddling through, of frenzied scrambling to catch up, of wasted efforts? If you have, a little planning, using precedent diagrams and time-scale charts, can prevent the recurrence of such nightmares.

But wait. We have talked only about tools for planning what is to be done. The tools are equally valuable for controlling the project while you are in the midst of it. Rarely will your progress unfold as planned; inevitably, delays and unforseen factors will necessitate altering even the best-laid plans. Maintain control. Use network charts to account for changes and make adjustments accordingly. Periodically redraw the charts in light of the changed status of parts of the project. Your charts will let you know where you are and how you should proceed to where you want to be. Use the diagram and chart to communicate with others. They promote understanding and support.

PERT/CPM

The precedent diagram and the time-scale chart belong to the general category of tools, "network techniques." Two earlier, well-known forerunners are PERT and CPM. Both use arrow diagrams and both are occasionally referred to as such. The PERT and CPM approaches do the same—no more—as precedent diagrams. PERT and CPM, however, involve unnecessary complexity, which necessitates nimble thinking. Today, project managers prefer precedent diagrams—and time-scale charts—the tools now at your disposal.

Network techniques will help you greatly, but they will not do the job for you. Plan your actions. Gain the understanding and support of everyone involved. Assume your responsibility, but maintain control primarily by knowing what's going on and anticipating the effects of what is happening.

5

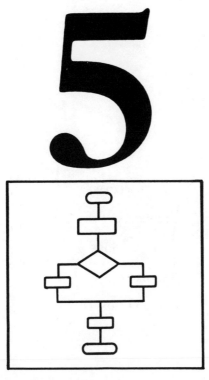

"Just Follow the Arrows"

OUTLINE
OF
CHAPTER
FIVE

{ ADP Flow-
charts

A PERSPECTIVE   { WHY A FLOWCHART?
                   AN EXAMPLE FLOWCHART
                   THE WRITTEN WORD

SYMBOLS

CONVENTIONS

LOOPING

CONCLUSION

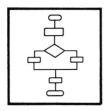

Why a flowchart?

When was the last time you thought through a procedure, described it to someone, or tried to write it out—a procedure that was somewhat complex because it involved several factors or variables, any one of which could cause a different set of steps? For many of us, this has happened frequently. We learn something new, we train others, or we wish to describe to others what *should happen.*

All right, we often go through such procedures, but how well or easily? Usually, quite poorly. When we reflect on the reasons why, the answer is obvious. If we are not, say, chess champions, or are intimately familiar with a situation, it is difficult to grasp everything that is involved. As we shall see, narrative descriptions of procedures also fail to present clearly even a moderately complex situation.

Enter upon the scene, the ADP flowchart. But what, you ask, is an ADP flowchart? Figure 1.2 entitled "How to Use This Book," is one such flowchart. A flowchart is a diagrammatic representation of the steps in a process or a procedure. If the flowchart is drawn correctly, its logic will be clear even to someone who is unfamiliar with the situation it portrays.

A sample flowchart

Figure 5.1 is another example, which shows an inventory-maintenance procedure.

This seems quite clear. Now suppose you were to prepare a job guide for this procedure, in *narrative* form, for a soon-to-arrive trainee who

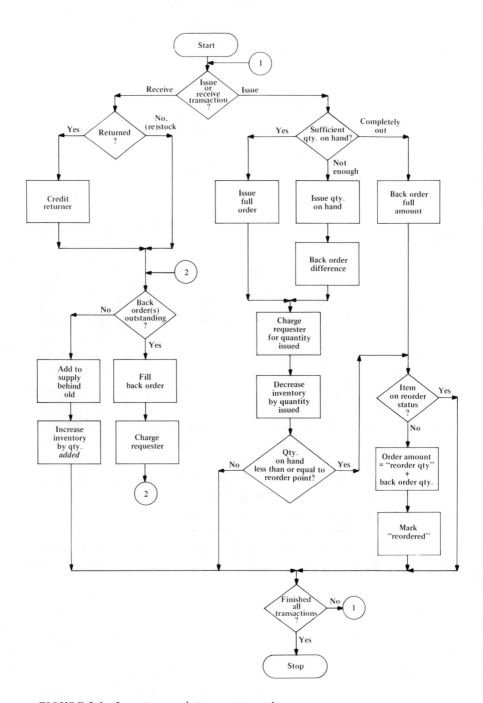

FIGURE 5.1: Inventory maintenance procedure

will handle this function. Could you do it? Even with Figure 5.1 as a guide, few of us are skillful enough to draft prose that is clear, accurate, and easily understood.

This situation is realistic. We must regularly communicate complex thoughts to others in a form more lasting than the spoken word, yet the written word fails us. Why? A newsletter published by a firm specializing in technical-writing consultation gives an answer. The newsletter says, in part:

> *Instructions frustrate us all. People who give us directions either tell us far more than we wanted to know or far too little. When people ask us for instructions, however, we inevitably feel we haven't provided the details most critical to their understanding.*
>
> *If someone asked us how to operate a manual [automobile] shift, for example, most of us would choose to show how to do it rather than write an explanation.*
>
> *The nature of the written word itself creates our most serious problems in instructions. Our minds can think of more than one thing at a time. Despite our intellectual sophistication, however, we must rely on a simple linear (or sequential) form for our instructions. We must read one word at a time, one sentence at a time. Regardless of the complexity of the processes we describe, the nature of the written language remains linear. And since we must use that linear format, we need to develop techniques that explain non-linear processes within those limits.*

This is precisely the problem. We do "need to develop techniques that explain non-linear processes"; but it is *not* necessary to use the linear format of writing. Flowcharts (and decision logic tables in the next chapter) help us break out of these limits. If you were learning the inventory maintenance procedure, wouldn't you prefer to use this flowchart over a written description?

Assuming that your answer is yes, let us move on to the ADP flowchart, beginning with the symbols. (ADP, which stands for *automatic data processing*, a type of flowchart, is a child of data processing.)

Symbols

Four simple figures make up the basic symbol set for ADP flowcharts. (Because they accomplish ninety-five percent of everything you need to describe, we omit mention of specialized symbols.) Inexpensive, commercially available templates make symbol drawing easy.

Symbol Name	Symbol	For . . .
Terminal		beginning and end of the logic flow
Process or "Do" Step		any action to be taken
Decision		any decision, test, or logical choice
Connector		showing that transfer to another point is appropriate and labeling the precise transfer point

FIGURE 5.2

The decision symbol necessitates additional comment. The symbol is used at any point where two or more logic paths begin. If more than three paths occur, use successive decision symbols to point the way, one pair at a time. To avoid ambiguity, label each exit branch from the diamond. See Figure 5.3.

Conventions

To achieve the greatest possible clarity, carefully follow these charting conventions:

The chart logic flows from top to bottom. Any variance must be clearly marked. Use arrowheads on flowlines to indicate direction.

Label all decision exits with the pertinent attribute.

Avoid crossing flowlines.

If branching or looping is needed, designate, using arrows or connectors, the precise point the logic flow should transfer to.

All logic flow emanates from one start symbol and terminates at a stop symbol (usually just one). This requires that no logic paths "dangle."

If necessary, predefined logic steps (called subroutines) can be referenced on another flowchart, or the process may be extended on one or more pages. Take care to annote your intent clearly to the reader.

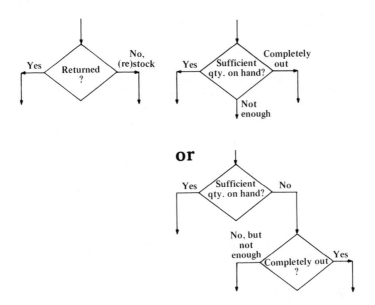

FIGURE 5.3

Looping

Looping is the branching back to a previous point to perform again instructions already stated. This obviates having to restate the instructions. Our sample flowchart contains two loops, one of which is reproduced in Figure 5.4.

Loops can be extremely advantageous. One must, however, pay strict attention to controlling the loop, that is, to controlling the number of passes through the loop. Figure 5.5 depicts a few variations, the first of which is an error that should be avoided.

Flowcharts are useful devices, which can be used to work through thought processes and thus avoid the pitfalls of written descriptions. Don't worry about neatness in the first drawing; concentrate on the logic. Then make a final, neat copy.

Flowcharts have some disadvantages, however. Once drawn, they can be difficult to change. Also, the more complex the situation—and therefore the chart—the more difficult it becomes to see what they portray. The user of the flowchart is likely to become lost in their logic. For these reasons, you may wish to use the Warnier diagram (Chapter 12) and/or the decision logic tables (Chap. 6)

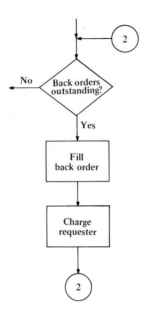

FIGURE 5.4

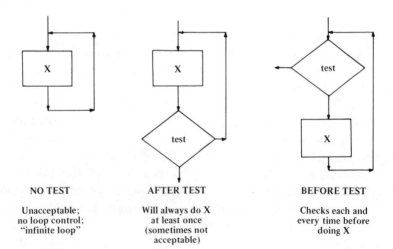

NO TEST	AFTER TEST	BEFORE TEST
Unacceptable; no loop control; "infinite loop"	Will always do X at least once (sometimes not acceptable)	Checks each and every time before doing X

FIGURE 5.5

6

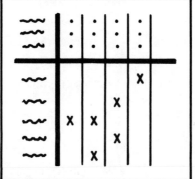

"Ask Me No Questions,
I'll Tell You No Lies"

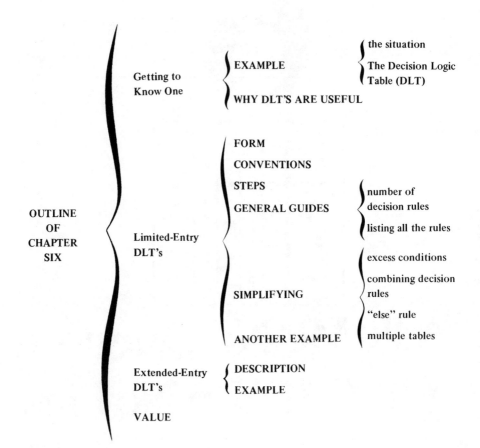

OUTLINE
OF
CHAPTER
SIX

Getting to
Know One

EXAMPLE

the situation

The Decision Logic
Table (DLT)

WHY DLT'S ARE USEFUL

Limited-Entry
DLT's

FORM

CONVENTIONS

STEPS

GENERAL GUIDES

number of
decision rules

listing all the rules

excess conditions

combining decision
rules

SIMPLIFYING

"else" rule

ANOTHER EXAMPLE

multiple tables

Extended-Entry
DLT's

DESCRIPTION

EXAMPLE

VALUE

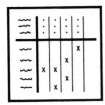

Getting to know one.

At this point you probably wouldn't know a decision logic table if you tripped over one, and maybe you think you wouldn't care. Chances are, though, you'd be glad to know about decision logic tables (DLT) if you faced a situation such as the following.

An example situation

An experienced bank teller needs to explain to a new trainee the bank's policy on cashing checks. This involves knowing the customers, whether checks are drawn on that bank, and the dollar amount of the checks. The teller uses this information to determine whether to check the account balance, require identification, get supervisory approval, and whether to infact cash the check or not.

How would you explain all this if you were the experienced teller? Write it out? If you did, it would probably read something like this:

> If the customer is known and has established an account with us, cash the check. Now here's what to do if the customer is not known. If the check is drawn on this bank, and is for an amount less than $51, cash the check. But if it's drawn on this bank, but is for $51 or more, check the balance in the account for sufficient funds before cashing the check. If the check is drawn on a different bank, and is for less than $51, the customer must show identification before we can cash the check.
>
> In the same situation, but for an amount of $51 or more, both proper identification and a bank officer's approval must precede cashing the check.

This is a typical description. Banks establish such guidelines to balance their risks with prompt service to customers. If you were the experienced teller, and were articulate enough to explain the bank's check-cashing policy, could you be sure that the trainee understood?

Assume that you *are* the trainee, that you have the above description in writing, and that you have time to study it. Could you follow the proper procedure in cashing a check for your first customer?

What, in fact, is the difficulty here? An ordinary situation appears to be muddled. Before we answer the question, let's look at a decision logic table, or DLT.

The decision logic table

Refer to table 6.1 as we discuss how to interpret a DLT. Each vertical column on the right of the table represents a possible situation. Read down the vertical columns to identify the situation and appropriate actions. Take the vertical column on the far right, for example. When the customer is not known, the check is not drawn on this bank, *and* the amount is more than $51, the teller must get the customer's identification and the approval of an officer before cashing the check.

Regardless of which teller you are, you should find the DLT easier than prose to comprehend or explain.

Why DLTs are useful

Let us return to the question about the difficulty. It involves three factors, five condition situations that could arise, and four possible courses of action. The difficulty lies in attempting to understand and express clearly the multiple combinations. Why is the decision logic table clearer? Because it lists, clearly and only once, the relevant conditions. Then the several decision rules are given straightforwardly, using the simple symbols, Y, N, and X. The DLT depicts the situation visually without the encumbrance of language. DLTs have other uses, which are discussed later.

Limited-entry DLTs

Decision logic tables appear in various forms. In this section the type used above is explained; after that, another form is shown. This form is known as a limited-entry decision logic table.

TABLE 6.1: Teller Guide for Cashing Checks.

	1	2	3	4	5
Known, established customer?	Y	N	N	N	N
Check drawn on this bank?	–	Y	Y	N	N
Amount less than $51?	–	Y	N	Y	N
Check account balance			X		
Require identification				X	X
Get supervisor's approval					X
Cash check*	X	X	X	X	X

*Assuming that all previous actions are satisfactory.

Form

In Table 6.1, the teller example, notice that double lines divide the DLT into four distinct parts. At the top left are conditions to be met or questions to be considered; the potential courses of action are at the bottom. At the top right are various possible circumstances that might arise and at the bottom right are the corresponding required actions. Figure 6.1 shows the IF, THEN relationship involved. The vertical columns on the right are called decision rules. Each decision rule specifies a particular set of conditions and the corresponding actions. A DLT may specify *actions* to be taken, or it may specify *results*–for example, action: cash check; result; credit limit: $1,200.

Conventions

You may already have guessed the limited-entry DLT conventions. They are:

A. Symbols

"Y"–yes; "N"–no; "-"–irrelevant (that is, ignore this condition);

"X"–take this action; " " [Blank] –do not take this action.

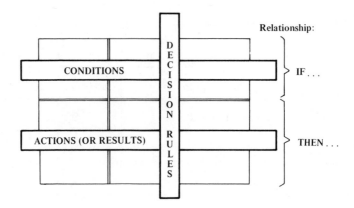

FIGURE 6.1: General form of decision logic tables.

B. Conditions

List each condition or question on a separate line. Although order is not crucial, place the governing, the most important, ones on top. (In our example, "know customer?" is placed on top because, if the answer is affirmative, other conditions may be ignored.)

C. Actions

List each action on a separate line.

List actions in the order in which they should be carried out; the DLT implies this sequence of actions.

D. Decision rules

Decision rules are numbered for ease of identification.

For completeness, have enough decision rules to cover all possible situations.

Usually, decision rules for the most commonly encountered situations are placed to the left in order to simplify use of the table.

Each rule is separate, independent of the others, and means this: *if* all the condition entries of a rule (the Y's and N's) are satisfied, *then* the indicated actions of that decision rule are done in sequence.

Steps

Using a limited-entry DLT is easy. Search for the vertical decision rule that matches, condition by condition, each aspect of a situation. Then perform, in sequence, the actions indicated for that decision rule.

When *creating* a DLT, expect to do it in rough form first, revise and simplify it, then to restate it in final form. Follow these general steps:

List all relevant conditions for factors in the upper left portion of the table.

List in the lower left portion all possible actions, from top to bottom, in the sequence they should follow.

Concerning decision rules: typically, the person creating the table drafts a rule for every possible condition, then combines, simplifies, and reorders the rules. By reordering, the rules most frequently encountered are placed on the left (see the general guidelines that follow).

Complete the decision rules generated by placing X's to indicate each appropriate action.

General guidelines

How do you know the proper number of a decision rules? By counting the number of applicable conditions. Let's call this number, n. Thus the maximum number of decision rules is 2^n. In the teller problem, three conditions apply; so $n = 3$. The maximum number of decision rules, therefore, is $2^n = 2^3 = 2 \times 2 \times 2 = 8$.

An easy way to list all possible combinations of condition sets is to study the pattern in Figure 6.2 and use it to generate your rules.

Create the pattern by following this approach carefully. For the first condition, mark (on the left) half the decision rules with Y's and (on

		half				half		
Condition # 1	Y	Y	Y	Y	N	N	N	N
		half		half				
Condition # 2	Y	Y	N	N	Y	Y	N	N
	half	half						
Condition # 3	Y	N	Y	N	Y	N	Y	N

FIGURE 6.2

the right) half with N's. For the second condition, look at the rules with Y's for the first condition; for these rules place Y's in the left half, and N's in the right. Proceed similarly for the rules having N's for condition one. Continue in this fashion for the remaining conditions. You have now generated all possible decision rules.

In summary, the aim here is to generate all possible decision rules. You can do this by filling in the Y's and N's by row, using the patterns described. Once this has been done, as in Figure 6.2, you can look down the vertical columns of each successive decision rule and see that each rule is different and that all possibilities have in fact been generated.

Simplifying

Excess conditions

Always try to simplify your table in each of the following ways. First, eliminate excess conditions. In the teller example, the condition "check drawn on another bank?" would be an excess condition that could be eliminated. Why? The answer to the question we did ask— "check drawn on this bank?"—also answers the excess question. Similarly, if we were testing for the colors of a stoplight, we would need to answer only two questions in order to tell which of the three possible colors it lit.

Combining decision rules

The check-cashing decision logic table is simplified by combining decision rules. With three conditions, there are $2^n = 2^3 = 8$ possible decision rules, as discussed above. Yet the example shows only five. The first rule—where the customer is, in fact, known and has established an account—combines four rules.

You can list the four decision rules by using the pattern method of generating all possible decision rules. Once the first condition is answered in the affirmative, the other two questions become irrelevant. The teller's action (cash the check) would be the same regardless of the other conditions. Asking these questions would be superfluous. Thus the rules are combined and hyphens are used to indicate the irrelevant questions: "check drawn on this bank?" and "amount less than $51".

A general guide for combining decision rules is: if two rules have exactly the same action or actions, and only one difference in their condition responses, they can be combined into one rule, with a hyphen for the condition where the difference is.

Figure 6.3 illustrates the guide as it applies to our example, where four rules are combined into one.

Figure 6.3 differs from the DLTs above, in that, here, one table is used to show three successive actions for combining rules. The middle part shows a stage where rules 1 and 2 have exactly the same actions and only one difference in their conditions. Thus the two rules are combined into one equivalent rule called A, which will replace rules 1 and 2. To the right of this, a similar action is depicted, which combines rules 3 and 4 to create a replacement rule—rule B. Finally, on the far right, rules A and B are restated together. They too may be combined for the same reason. The result is rule C, which, in effect, replaces rules 1 through 4.

ELSE rule

The ELSE rule offers a way to simplify a DLT; it amounts to a catch-all decision rule placed at the far right of the table.

Figure 6.4 illustrates the ELSE rule. Here, rules 1, 2, and 3 are only three of the eight possibilities that can arise from three conditions. The ELSE rule serves as a substitute for all otherwise missing decision rules (here, five). In any situation not covered by rules 1, 2, or 3, the supervisor must be called.

When is the ELSE rule used? Generally, you might apply the rule when (1) you wish to keep the number of decision rules to a minimum, (2) when there is little chance of a situation occurring, or (3) when only some of the possible situations require testing.

Multiple tables

One way to simplify a large DLT is to break it up into smaller tables. The reader of split tables should first be directed to the overall table and second, as a final action of each table, told where to go next.

The ADP flowchart in Figure 5.1 illustrates an inventory maintenance procedure. This flowchart can be converted, as can any flowchart, to a decision logic table.

One DLT for the entire process of describing both "receive" and "issue" transactions would be unwieldy. The solution is to create two separate tables, one for handling receive transactions and the other for

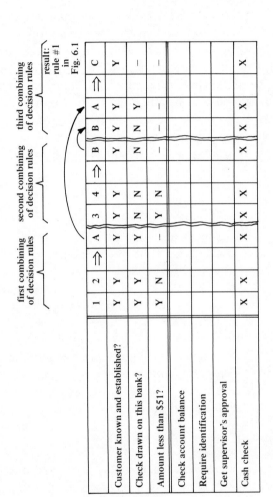

FIGURE 6.3

Example of ELSE Rule

	1	2	3	ELSE
Condition A?	Y	Y	N	
" B?	Y	N	Y	
" C?	–	Y	N	
Action X	X		X	
Action Y		X	X	
Call Supervisor				X

FIGURE 6.4

handling issue transactions. In a section below, this same inventory example is used for multiple tables.

You will have to use your judgment as to when multiple tables are advisable. Generally (without an ELSE rule), a situation with more than four conditions (that is, up to sixteen decision rules) becomes unmanageable, and multiple tables should be considered.

Another example

Table 6.2 provides another illustration of a limited-entry decision logic table. For the reader's convenience, decision rules 1 and 2, which represent the situations most often encountered, are placed at the left. Rule 3 is a combination of the other possible rules. Here, if the received items are not ordered, the other conditions are irrelevant, and the received shipment should be refused. All other possible decision rules are replaced by the ELSE rule. The table originator apparently felt that either few such situations would occur or that the judgment of those in authority should be applied rather than taking a predefined action. With the ELSE rule added, all conditions are covered. The rest of the table is self-explanatory.

Extended-entry DLTs

Decision logic tables take many forms. Another type, called the extended-entry DLT, should be in your toolbox. It is useful in situations where some conditions may have many variables. Table 6.3 is a simple DLT of this type.

Notice that the entire horizontal line is needed to define both the conditions and the actions. Such a table saves space.

Let's look at a more realistic example. Remember in Figure 5.1 the statement that the inventory maintenance procedure can be described in terms of decision logic tables. In using the procedure for handling issue transactions, one must, if possible, fill the request, back order when necessary, keep the inventory current, and reorder if necessary. This is illustrated in Table 6.4 and Table 6.5. The first, "Handling Issue Transactions," is an example of the extended-entry form. The second, "Reorder Table," is "mixed entry" because of its hybrid form, a mixture of limited-entry and extended-entry formats.

Value of decision logic tables

Decision logic tables can:

Display an entire situation visually, with alternatives shown side by side.

Force the table creator to examine a procedure carefully.

Aid in ensuring that all situations are actively considered.

Direct the reader to precisely what is needed thus (the reader is not likely to become bogged down in information not pertinent to the immediate need).

Greatly aid communication by promoting understanding and reducing misunderstanding.

Where can you use decision logic tables? Next time you find yourself writing narrative descriptions of procedures or results that involve various conditions, stop; you may have before you a good opportunity to use DLTs.

TABLE 6.2: Instructions for receiving shipments

	1	2	3	ELSE
Were received items ordered?	Y	Y	N	
Correct quantity received?	Y	N	–	
Are received items damaged?	N	N	–	
Have carrier attest (in writing) as to quantity		X		
Accept shipment	X	X		
Refuse shipment			X	
Call chief of purchasing				X

TABLE 6.3: Assigning credit ratings

	1	2	3	4
Debts paid	on time	on time	late	late
Employment pattern	steady	intermittent	steady	intermittent
Assign credit rating	excellent	good	fair	poor

TABLE 6.4: Handling "issue" transactions

	1	2	3
Quantity on hand	enough	*not* enough	out
Issue	qty. requested	qty. on hand	
Charge requester for	qty. issued	qty. issued	
Decrease inventory by	qty. issued	qty. issued	
Back order		difference	qty. requested
Go next to	Reorder table	Reorder table	Reorder table

TABLE 6.5: Reorder table

	1	2	3
Is inventory now below reorder point?	Y	Y	N
Is item already reordered?	Y	N	–
Reorder		the "Reorder Quantity"	
Mark as		"Reordered"	
Handle next transaction	X	X	X

7

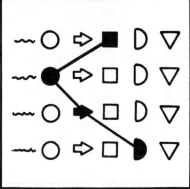

"Let It Flow,
Let It Flow,
Let It Flow"

OUTLINE OF CHAPTER SEVEN

- **Making It Simple**
  - SUBJECT OF CHAPTER (4 CHARTS)
  - PARTS OF CHAPTER
  - USES OF CHAPTER
    - Approach for Each
      - learning
      - using

- **Kinds of Charts**
  - GENERAL DISCUSSION

- **Chart Selector Guide**

- **("How To's" of Each Chart)**
  - **WORKFLOW CHART**
    - purpose
    - form
    - convention
    - examples
  - **DOCUMENT DISTRIBUTION CHART**
    - purpose
    - symbols
    - conventions
    - form/example
  - **PROCESS CHART**
    - purpose
    - symbols
    - conventions
    - form
      - single column
      - multiple column
  - **PROCEDURE CHART**
    - purpose
    - symbols
    - convention
    - form: an example
    - steps

- **The Six Step Method**
  - Pick a situation (to improve)
  - Choose the chart
  - Collect the data
  - Analyze the results
  - Develop an improved process
  - Install the new process

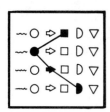

Making it simple.

Nearly everyone works or participates in an *organization*. We employ this term loosely, for most of us are not well organized. Why? Possibly because our structure ill suits the processes in our organization, or because our processes are not structured. Perhaps we do not understand our organization's processes, or structure, or both.

In every organization, to facilitate work, materials (especially paper) must flow between people and units. To better organize this flow, one improves the flow of work, materials, and paper. How, you may ask. Our "toolbox" contains four handy tools: (1) workflow charts, (2) document-distribution charts, (3) process charts, and (4) procedure charts. This chapter acquaints you with each tool, guides your choice of tools, and instructs you in the application—all so you can understand, describe, and improve the process in your organization. And, in turn, become better organized.

This chapter is divided into the following distinct parts:

Kind of chart—to provide perspective

Chart selector—to guide your choice of tools

The how-to's of each chart—to describe them in detail

The "six-step method"—to make you skilled in applying the charts

Basically, use of this chapter should vary, depending on your purpose— understanding or using the tools. Table 7.1 suggests an alternate sequence of sections for either purpose.

TABLE 7.1:

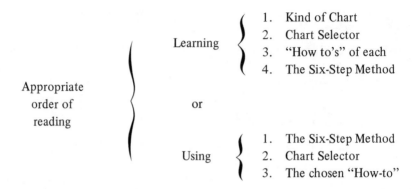

Kinds of charts

We have stated our purpose as improving the flow of organizational processes. Different charting techniques exist because people have adopted different viewpoints from which to study the flow. The four chosen for this chapter allow a choice of viewpoints. Predicate your choice of tool on basic viewpoints—for example: What flow do I want to study? Is the flow of a single item? Is it a simple or a complex flow? Do I want to know in general or in detail what is happening? Which do I care more about—*what* is done or *where* (or, by whom) it is done? The four charts differ precisely according to these qualities.

Do *not* make your selection on the basis of the chart's *name*. The names are a major source of confusion. Because we must, however, distinguish among the four, we have adopted the commonly accepted nomenclature.

Chart selector guide

Select the chart that is appropriate for the purpose or purposes you have in mind. As an aid, refer to Figure 7.1, the "Chart Selector Guide." Determine which chart form most closely corresponds to your needs, then turn to the appropriate how-to material. What follows is a how-to description of the four chart forms.

TO STUDY OR SHOW:		LIKE THIS:	WHICH IS:	THEN SEE:
Overview of & What happens	Where it's done		WORK FLOW CHART	Page 92
Paperwork &	Where it goes		DOCUMENT DISTRIBUTION CHART	Page 93
Detail steps of a relatively simple situation (one person or paper) &	What happens - OR - What happens and where (or by whom)		Single Column } PROCESS CHART	Page 93, 94
			Multiple Column	Page 93, 98
Detail steps of a Complex Situation (e.g. multiple papers)			Multi-Column PROCEDURE CHART	Page 98 *Note:* requires doing PROCESS CHARTS first

FIGURE 7.1: Chart selector guide.

Workflow charts

Workflow charts usually provide a bird's-eye view, as opposed to a detailed one. They display the sequence of major operational steps and the organizational units performing the steps. (If you wish, substitute the major phases of the work flow for the organizational units.) The general purpose of the chart is quickly inferred from its form. Figure 7.2 shows the layout of a workflow chart.

Conventions

Create your chart in the following conventional manner:

1. Label organizational units across the top. Order is not crucial, although a clean appearance suggests placement and thus minimizes zig-zagging of the flowline.

2. List major operational steps on the left in chronological sequence, from top to bottom.

3. For each step, place a dot in the cell that corresponds to the unit performing the work.

4. Draw a flowline that will connect the dots in sequence.

See Figure 1.3, "Guide for the Timid," which is actually a version of the workflow chart. A workflow chart conveniently depicts the overall process of procurement (see Fig. 7.3). Below, we look at some of the complexities behind this simplified view.

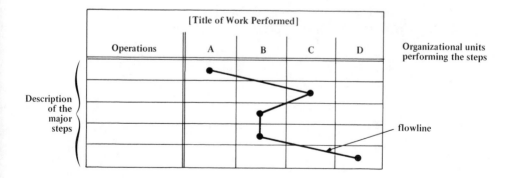

FIGURE 7.2: Form of workflow charts

OVERVIEW OF THE PROCUREMENT PROCESS			
Steps	User Division	Finance	Purchasing
Request purchase	●		
Approve funding		●	
Initiate procurement			●
Receive and inspect			●
Receive item	●		
Disburse payment		●	

FIGURE 7.3

Document-distribution charts

Document-distribution charts usually depict the flow of multiple copies of a form or a document through either organizational units or major processing stages. Its use is restricted to overview statements of the processing. For a more detailed expression, consider the multicolumn procedure chart. The basic symbols used in the document-distribution chart consist of only a few simple figures. See Figure 7.4.

Three conventions foster understanding: (1) flow is generally left to right and top to bottom, but it is always clarified by arrowheads on the flowlines; (2) the flow of each document, or copy thereof, is shown; and (3) a brief description of the processing involved is usually added near most symbols. The document-distribution chart is illustrated in Figure 7.5, "Procurement System." Feel free to vary the form of this or any chart; no format is inviolate.

Process charts

If you want to study in detail what happens in a relatively simple situation involving a single document, a material, or even the actions of a person, consider the process chart. Defining a "relatively simple situation" is not practical; instead familiarize yourself with the multicolumn procedure chart for *complex* situations. Then exercise your judgment as to which is the most appropriate tool.

The process chart documents the detailed steps of the flow and categorizes the type of action taken. With this information, you can subsequently analyze the process for potential improvements.

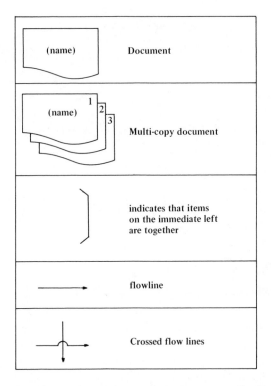

FIGURE 7.4: Symbols used in document-distribution charts

The type of action involved in each step is classified by one of five standard symbols—operation, transportation, inspection, delay, or storage (Fig. 7.6). Every action is recorded, using one of these symbols. These actions, or steps, are recorded in chronological order. A flowline connects the symbols, thus highlighting the sequence.

Single-column format

You may encounter two forms of the process chart—the single-column format and the multicolumn format. The single-column format utilizes a form having preprinted action symbols. As each step is listed (vertically, in chronological order), the user shades in the appropriate symbol and, with a flowline, connects the symbol to the preceding one. Figure 7.7 is an example of the single-column process chart used to document the steps in a purchase-order request. Figure 7.7 gives the specifics generalized in the document-distribution chart shown in Figure 7.5. The chart reveals a lengthy process for what appears to be a simplistic situation.

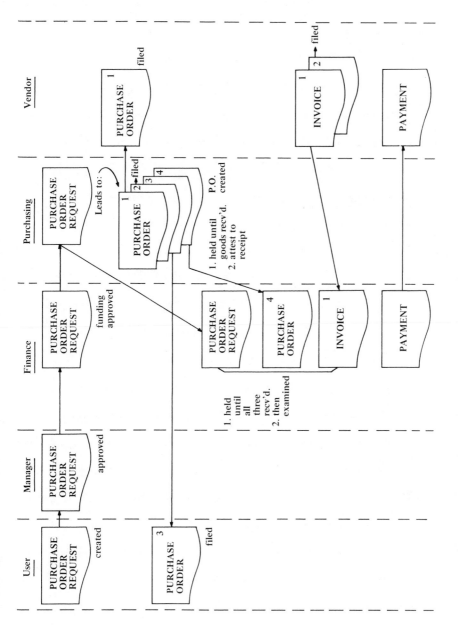

FIGURE 7.5: Procurement system: document distribution chart

○	**OPERATION**	When something is *CHANGED or CREATED*
		for example:
		  - altered in any way
		  - prepared for another action
		  - calculations are made
		  - information is given or received

⇨	**TRANSPORTATION**	When something is *MOVED*
		for example:
		  - from one place to another
		  - but if movement is inherent in an operation of another kind, the action is *not* labeled as transportation

☐	**INSPECTION**	When something is *VERIFIED* or checked for example: examined for quality, quantity, accuracy, completeness, special characteristics

D	**DELAY**	When something *WAITS*
		for example:
		  - for the next planned action
		  - due to backlog
		  - due to unplanned break in the flow

▽	**STORAGE**	When something is *KEPT*
		for example:
		  - filed
		  - secured
		(Occasionally the triangle is shaded in to represent permanent storage.)

FIGURE 7.6: Process chart symbols.

(Single-Column)
PROCESS CHART

Number of steps of
each type of action

JOB: Tracking a Purchase Order Request in the Procurement Cycle

☐ Person   or ■ Material: Purchase Order Request

■ Present   or ☐ Proposed Procedure

○	OPERATIONS	5
⇨	TRANSPORTATIONS	4
☐	INSPECTIONS	4
D	DELAYS	8
▽	STORAGES	2

STEPS OF (☐ PRESENT / ☐ PROPOSED) METHOD — OPERATION / TRANSPORT. / INSPECTION / DELAY / STORAGE — NOTES

Step	Description	Operation	Transport	Inspection	Delay	Storage
1	User creates purchase order request	●	⇨	☐	D	▽
2	User puts in Out basket	○	⇨	☐	●	▽
3	Taken to manager	○	◆	☐	D	▽
4	Placed in In basket	○	⇨	☐	●	▽
5	Manager examines	○	⇨	■	D	▽
6	Manager approves	●	⇨	☐	D	▽
7	Manager places in Out basket	○	⇨	☐	●	▽
8	Taken to Finance	○	◆	☐	D	▽
9	Placed in In basket	○	⇨	☐	●	▽
10	Accountant examines	○	⇨	■	D	▽
11	Accountant approves funding	●	⇨	☐	D	▽
12	Accountant places in Out basket	○	⇨	☐	●	▽
13	Taken to Purchasing	○	◆	☐	D	▽
14	Placed in In basket	○	⇨	☐	●	▽
15	Procurement clerk examines	○	⇨	■	D	▽
16	Procurement clerk uses to create **P.O.**	●	⇨	☐	D	▽
17	Procurement clerk places in Out basket	○	⇨	☐	●	▽
18	Taken to Finance	○	◆	☐	D	▽
19	Placed in In basket	○	⇨	☐	●	▽
20	Accountant places in pending file	○	⇨	☐	D	▼
21	Accountant (later) retrieves file	●	⇨	☐	D	▽
22	Accountant examines	○	⇨	■	D	▽
23	Accountant files permanently	○	⇨	☐	D	▼
24		○	⇨	☐	D	▽

FIGURE 7.7: Single-Column process chart

Multicolumn format

The second form of the process chart drops the verbal descriptors of the steps but differentiates graphically among the people involved. Figure 7.8 represents the purchase-order-request situation. No column exists for explanation; key words are simply added near the symbols. The figure is a "horizontal multicolumn chart"; a vertical variation is the source of the descriptive name, *multicolumn*.

A process chart both documents the current situation and opens the way for analysis aimed at improvement. In the single-column chart, the form itself contains sections intended for analysis of the flow described. The multicolumn chart (Fig. 7.9) furnishes tips for analysis. For additional guidance, see also the section, "Six-Step Method" below.

Procedure charts

As valuable as these three chart forms are, they are inadequate in tackling large, complex situations. However, we do have available the multicolumn procedure chart, a tool that enables us to display, in detail, several processes occurring simultaneously—for example, the actions of two or more people or the flow of multiple, interacting documents. Because its very power is intended to display complex situations, the multicolumn procedure chart is more complex than the other charts we have discussed.

PURCHASE ORDER REQUEST (P.O.R.)

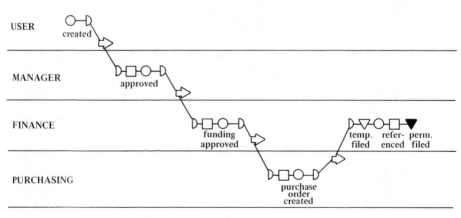

FIGURE 7.8: Multi-Column process chart

IN LOOKING AT THE WHOLE CHART, WATCH FOR TROUBLE AREAS SUCH AS THESE:

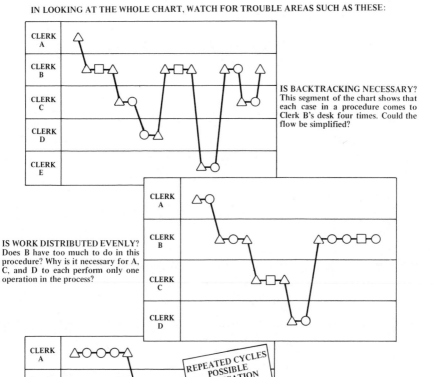

IS BACKTRACKING NECESSARY? This segment of the chart shows that each case in a procedure comes to Clerk B's desk four times. Could the flow be simplified?

IS WORK DISTRIBUTED EVENLY? Does B have too much to do in this procedure? Why is it necessary for A, C, and D to each perform only one operation in the process?

IS THERE DUPLICATION? Could the sequence or cycle of steps performed by B, C, and D be performed once only? To answer all questions such as these, further study is needed.

FIGURE 7.9: Sighting targets for improvement

Yet three factors should alay any apprehension of this chart form. First, the symbols are easy to understand. Second, separate (single-column) process charts are coalesced to create this chart. Third, you would normally be applying this tool to a situation which you are already familiar with. So let's proceed by discussing—in order—the symbols, conventions, an example, and finally, the steps. Familiarize yourself with the explanations of the basic symbols in Figure 7.10 and the secondary symbols in Figure 7.11.

Conventions

The procedure chart uses a horizontal row for each document (copy, person, or material). In general, one places on the row all actions affecting that item, allowing sufficient space between lines to avoid confusion. The standard symbols may be augmented with key words or annotations as needed.

Form

We need an example at this point. The requisition system mentioned above will suffice. Figure 7.5 gives us an overall view of the process. Figure 7.7 is then used to detail the actions affecting the purchase-order request. Similar process charts for the other documents are not presented here. Since their steps are quite simple, we skip directly to the procedure chart. To conserve space, let the procedure chart pick

OPERATION	⊙ to **CREATE** one or more documents
	Ⓐ to **ADD** information
	◯ to **HANDLE** a document
INSPECTION	☐ to examine, check, or verify a document
TRANSPORTATION	▷ to **MOVE** from one place or another
DELAY	D to **WAIT**
STORAGE	▽ temporary
	▼ permanent

FIGURE 7.10: Basic symbols for procedure charts

Symbol	Description	Example
RELATED or ATTACHED	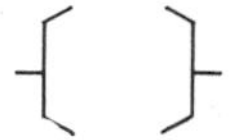 Shows items are together and/or treated the same.	e.g., 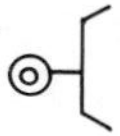 Copy 1 / Copy 2 — Create two together
ONE FORM AFFECTING ANOTHER	 The "V" may go up or down.	e.g., 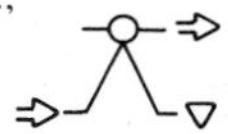 The lower affects the higher
SIMULTANEOUS ACTION	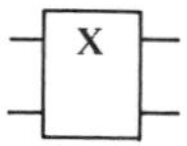 The appropriate action symbol is placed where the X is.	e.g., 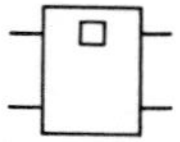 both inspected simultaneously
ALTERNATE ACTION	 Used when processing may be in different ways. Straight line assumed to be normal processing. Raised (or lowered) to be the exception.	e.g., 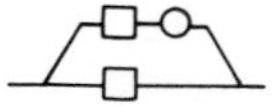 normally just inspect
SKIPPING	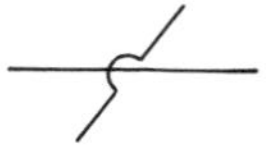 Usually used with second symbol above. Needed because it is often not possible to put related documents on adjacent lines.	e.g., 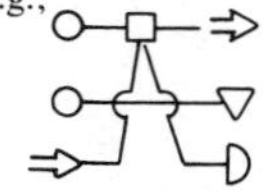 bottom affects the top but not the middle
OMITTED	References a series of operations performed elsewhere; used when detail of operations is not necessary.	e.g., repaired by service firm

FIGURE 7.11: Secondary symbols for procedure charts

up at the point where the purchase-order request arrives at the purch-asing department. For clarity, and to facilitate comparison with Figure 7.13, Figure 7.5 is reproduced as Figure 7.12.

Spend some time familiarizing yourself with Figure 7.13. It contains all the basic and secondary symbols. By doing this, you should be able to create a multicolumn procedure chart for use in other situations.

Steps

Three phases lead to the creation of a procedure chart:

1. Mentally establish the boundaries of the situation to be sur-veyed. What is and what is not within the "domain of inquiry"? For example, what forms, people, or materials are involved? We will call these boundaries *items*.

2. Using the single-column *process* chart, track separately the flow of each item selected.

3. Figuratively speaking, place these *process* charts alongside one another, on their sides. (Remember, a process chart tracks the detail steps of a single document, using a column of preprinted symbols.)

Imagine turning a process chart on its side; the result is a sequence of steps along a horizontal line. Redraft each process chart along a horizontal line of the *procedure* chart. Proper alignment reflects the relationship and interaction of the separate items, each of which is on a separate line. Concentrate on the main procedure of the problem de-fined, omitting extraneous branches.

The six-step method

In the sections above we cover the how-to's of each kind of chart. You may have just read those sections, or perhaps you skipped directly to here because you were familiar with the material in them. Knowledge of the charts, however, does not necessarily prepare you for analyzing situations and making improvements. To assist you in that, we examine an approach called the six-step method.

The six-step method is a rational, analytical approach to applying the process charts. But don't take the opposite approach. You needn't memorize the method or apply it methodically. Peruse it first; that

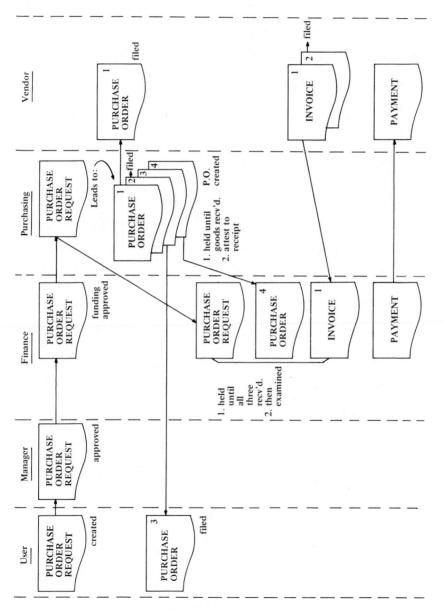

FIGURE 7.12: Procurement system: document distribution chart

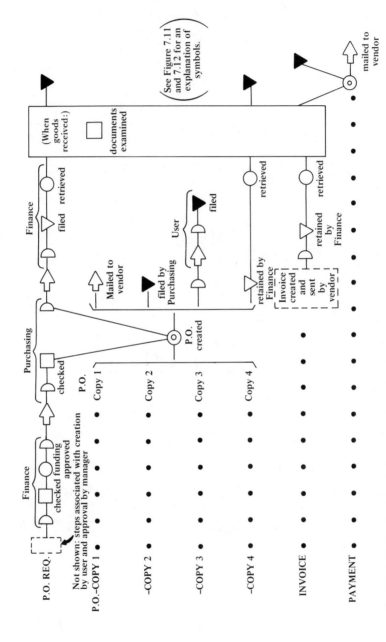

FIGURE 7.13: Multi-column procedure chart for procurement system

way, you will be more likely to glean some ideas. Select, say, three ideas from the method and incorporate them in your own approach.

The six steps, in order, are:

1. Pick a situation to improve.

2. Choose a chart.

3. Collect the data.

4. Analyze the results.

5. Devise an improved process.

6. Install the process.

Listed so flatly, the steps might initially be ignored. Review the points listed below, however; they can make your task easier.

1. Pick a situation to improve.

a. Refer to Chapter 2 for the Pareto principle if you've not heard of it.

b. Look at the repetitive processes; they are analyzable and can offer big dividends. Office work is fertile ground for improvement possibilities. Periods of major change are opportunities to use these tools.

c. Look at the overview first, before going into detail. Can the whole thing be eliminated? If so, throw it away; don't try to fix it.

d. Lay the groundwork. Be sure the way is clear and that all interested parties are aware of your effort. Solicit their help.

2. Choose a chart.

a. See the chart-selection guide.

b. If what you need is not there, create what you need—a chart form of your own.

3. Collect the data.

Collecting data is a lot like collecting garbage—you've got to know what you're going to do with the stuff before you collect it.

— Mark Twain

All the following apply:

Document what is actually being done, not what should be done or what someone thinks should be done.

Describe each step even though it might appear minor.

Concentrate on the main flow of work, relating exceptions or variations to this flow.

4. Analyze the results.

a. Study your as-is chart, the one you made depicting the current situation.

b. First, look at the entire chart.

Symptom	*Implied possibilities*
backtracking	improper distribution of functions
repeated cycles of steps	overlapping or duplication
bottlenecks	unwarranted delays, too many interruptions
rows (on multicolumn process chart) nearly empty.	uneven distribution of work

c. Second, look at *groups* of steps. Question their collective purpose, sequence, and placement, as well as the need for them.

d. Third, look at the *individual* steps. For each, ask whether it can be eliminated, combined, simplified, or improved in sequence.

5. Devise an improved process.

One pound of learning requires ten pounds of common sense to apply it.

—Persian proverb

The people involved with the flow usually know how to improve it. Learn from them. They are crucial to this and other stages.

6. Install the process.

a. You must not attempt this independently or unilaterally. Others must support the change if it is to succeed.

b. People resist change because it disrupts their work habits, disturbs their complacency and inertia, implies criticism, and affects their perceptions of security. In step 5 above, when you devised an improved process, you addressed the need for "technological" change. Now we address the issue of social change. Enlist the participation of everyone involved; it's the key to acceptance of change. In general, keep an open mind, maintain a questioning attitude, and solicit teamwork.

To repeat, these tools are well suited to documenting, improving, and standardizing procedures, to training and orienting personnel, to making notes of your observations, and to communicating with others. Add them to your toolbox.

8

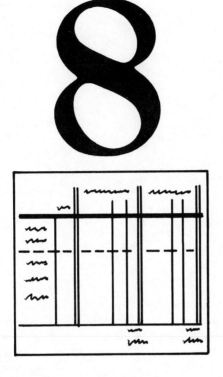

"Enie Menie,–"

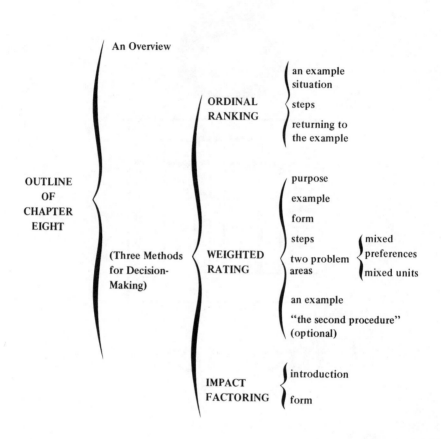

OUTLINE
OF
CHAPTER
EIGHT

An Overview

(Three Methods
for Decision-
Making)

ORDINAL
RANKING

an example
situation

steps

returning to
the example

WEIGHTED
RATING

purpose

example

form

steps

two problem
areas

mixed
preferences
mixed units

an example

"the second procedure"
(optional)

IMPACT
FACTORING

introduction

form

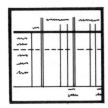

Overview

How do you make decisions? Do you use your intuition, choose what "feels right," read tea leaves, seek someone else's opinion, scientifically evaluate the information available? There is no single right way; different situations call for different approaches. Sometimes a popular, informal method is as good as any of the others: use a portable, binary, solid-state decision maker—that is, flip a coin.

This chapter does not disparage any of the above methods of decision-making; rather, my aim is to offer new approaches. The focal point is decision-making in which a *single decision* must be made based on a choice among several alternatives. Situations of multiple or sequential decisions are addressed in Chapter 9.

Three techniques are presented in the order, ordinal ranking, weighted rating, and impact factoring. A particular situation dictates the technique that is most useful. In short, consider ordinal ranking when you are not sure about the order of preferences among choices, where one or no criterion for the choice is involved; consider weighted rating or impact factoring when the choice is to be based on several criteria.

Ordinal ranking

An illustration is the best introduction. Picture a wholesale buyer of clothing who successfully anticipates the tastes of the buying public, thus the marketability of certain styles, six to nine months before the styles become popular. On one particular day, the buyer has sorted through some 150 sample suits and narrowed the selection to six of similar styling. Each suit would be a good choice, but only two are needed. After weeding out 144 suits, our buyer is gripped by indecision. Which two of the six equally acceptable suits should be chosen? Ordinal ranking helps the buyer order the preferences among the six items.

The following, simple steps are used to make a selection:

1. Arbitrarily order the choices: A, B, C, and so on.

2. Create a triangular matrix as follows:
   a. Down the left side, from the top, list each element except the last in arbitrary order and label as —A, B, C.
   b. Across the top, from the left, list the elements in reverse order, starting with the last but omitting the first element. (e.g., E, D, C, and B.)

3. For each square, compare the appropriate two items. Starting at the top, proceed across the row, comparing the item on the left with that on the top. Determine your preference between the two, and write the choice in the square. (For example, in the upper left most square of figure 8.1). Don't skip any squares; if you can't decide, write in either one. Continue recording your preferences for all squares.

4. Now apart from the triangle diagram you've been using, make three columns. In the first column, the one on the left, list the alternatives in the initial, arbitrary order. In the second column, record for each alternative the frequency of that alter-

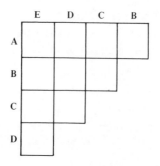

FIGURE 8.1: Ordinal ranking matrix (for six items)

native *in all the squares of the matrix*. For example, tally the number of times A occurs in the squares and record this number in the second column. In the third column, "Ranking," write in "1" for the alternative with the highest frequency (listed in the middle column). Assign "2" to the alternative with the second greatest frequency. Continue this process for alternatives listed in column one.

5. You now have, in the third column, a ranking of preference among the alternatives. Note, however, that you must not assume a degree of preference between any two items. For example, it is incorrect to conclude that A is three times better than C, because A occurs in the matrix three times as often as C, or because A has a rank of, say, 2, and C's rank is 6; relative degrees of preference are not determinable with ordinal ranking.

Our buyer cannot decide among the six suits, which we will label A, B, C, D, and E. The buyer quickly draws the ordinal ranking matrix and successively compares each pair of jackets. The result of this procedure is shown in Figure 8.2.

The buyer tallies the frequency with which each item occurs in the matrix (see Table 8.1). In order of frequency are D and F, C, E, and A and B. Note the two ties: D occurs as often as F and A as often as B. This, however, does not disturb the buyer, who ranks them as shown in the table.

	F	E	D	C	B
A	F	E	D	C	A
B	F	E	B	C	
C	F	C	D		
D	D	D			
E	F				

FIGURE 8.2: Matrix

TABLE 8.1: Ordinal ranking of six suits

Alternative	Frequency in Matrix	Ranking
A	1	5
B	1	6
C	3	3
D	4	1
E	2	4
F	4	2

The buyer rank ordered the suits, D, F, C, E, A, B. Note that D is arbitrarily ranked ahead of F and A ahead of B. This should be acceptable for the ranking, because (1) the buyer is indifferent between two alternative suits having the same frequency and (2) the ordering at the beginning was arbitrary. Since the buyer must select two styles, the choices are D and F.

Look back over the process, it's really simple. One makes the decision by using a series of pair comparisons, tallying the results and ranking the alternatives, based on the tally made. Remember that it is incorrect to read from this a degree of relative preference among the choices.

Weighted rating method

Now we explore a different kind of situation, one often faced by decision-makers. Again, it is a matter of making one decision. Here, though, the factors on which to base a decision differ. The decision-maker must choose among alternatives where several factors, called criteria, must be considered. If viewed separately, the criteria might suggest different selections. The decision-maker thus has a problem.

In an example explained below, a store owner is about to remodel, prior to the arrival of goods purchased by the buyer discussed above. The owner faces a choice of one of three models of garment racks. The factors affecting the selection are cost, capacity, compatibility with decor, and delivery time. How should the decision-maker make a choice, considering that each criterion may dictate a different choice?

An intuitive or subjective decision is not necessarily a bad one. But, to clarify the decision process, and, if need be, to back up a decision, use the weighted rating method. Weighted rating can guide you through the decision-making process by showing you how to list the relevant criteria and how to weigh each criterion according to its relative importance. Evaluate the alternatives, using the criteria. Then, with elementary arithmetic, use a point system to rate each alternative and thus compare alternatives.

Table 8.2 is an example of a simplified format and the arithmetic procedure to be used. Accept the weights and ratings as given, but note how the weighted ratings are calculated. In this case, since large numbers are preferred to small ones, the choice indicated is alternative Y.

Like all the tools in this book, weighted rating uses a chart format. Here, though, the form of the chart is unimportant; the chart should be used merely to guide the process. Figure 8.3, with annotations, represents the format typical of weighted-rating charts.

Steps

The steps involved in the weighted rating method are listed here with little explanation. The reader is warned not to follow these steps without reading the next section, which contains a discussion of two im-

TABLE 8.2: *An example of weighted ratings*

		Alternative X		Alternative Y	
Criteria	Wt.*	Rate*	Wt. x Rate	Rate*	Wt x Rate
Criterion 1	10	5	50	8	80
Criterion 2	4	6	24	2	8
Criterion 3	7	9	63	8	63
Totals	–	–	137	–	151

Here high numbers are preferred.

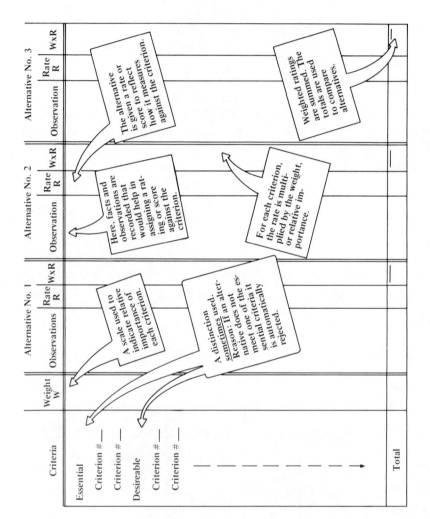

FIGURE 8.3: General form of matrix for weighted rating.

portant problem areas. The example that then follows serves as an explanation of the steps:

1. Identify each alternative choice.

2. List the criteria, factors, and considerations that are the basis of the decision. Examples are: cost, availabiltiy, side effects, acceptability, and so on. Those criteria that are crucial (as opposed to merely desirable) should be denoted; see Figure 8.3. Then any alternative not satisfying an essential criterion is to be rejected, regardless of other considerations.

3. Rate each alternative against each criterion. Two points are worth mentioning:
   a. The example below demonstrates two ways of assigning numerical ratings; a third way is offered here: the decision maker may find that the rating process is made easier by first assigning a verbal category—for example, excellent or good—and then converting the category to a number. A typical equivalence is: excellent, 4; very good, 3; good, 2; fair, 1; poor, 0.
   b. Do read the important section entitled "Two Problem Areas."

4. Multiply the criterion weight by the rating, to get a weighted rating for the alternative for that criterion.

5. For each alternative, sum up the weighted ratings to calculate a total score.

6. Compare the alternatives, using their total scores.

Two Problem Areas

In using the weighted rating method, you must be aware of issues that cause problems if not handled properly—"mixed preferences" and "mixed units." Once you know what these are, and how to deal with them, you should have no trouble. Both are, to some extent, explained below. The example that follows completes the explanation.

Problem area: mixed preferences

In the weighted rating method, points are assigned to an alternative for each criterion; then the points are added, yielding a total score. Some attributes are favorable, and some are not. For example, *low* cost is desirable, whereas *low* holding capacity is not. This mixing of preferences is a source of confusion and trouble.

For the weighted method to make sense, you must first determine whether you prefer high numbers or low numbers; then you must make sure that the rating assigned reflects this preference. For example, say that you choose a scale of 1 to 10 for your ratings, where 10 is the highest valued rating (that is, large numbers are preferred). For cost, then, you will want to assign a *high* score—say, 9 or 10—to the alternative with the *lowest* cost. If low cost is desirable, you will choose high numbers, assigning a high number where the cost is low. Let us assume that your choice is among three racks: chrome, at $425; oak, at $390; and avant-garde, at $495. The low-priced oak rack receives a 10, the highest rating. For holding capacity, however, the rack with the highest capacity receives the highest rating.

For the method to work, you must first determine which you prefer, high or low numbers. Then you must examine each criterion for desirability (or undesirability) before assigning a rating. Attempt to assign ratings in proportion to the relative desirability of the alternatives. The following example will help clarify this point.

Problem area: mixed units

The old adage about adding apples and oranges applies equally to the weighted rating method. Most criteria involve some units of measure. For example:

criteria	measure
cost	dollars
holding capacity	items per square foot of floor space
delivery time	weeks

With different units, these measures cannot be summed meaningfully. Because the weighted rating method is predicated on adding the ratings of all criteria, something must be done to address this problem. Two procedures are commonly used.

The first procedure eliminates the units by converting the value having units (for example, dollars or weeks) to a unitless scale. Here, choose a scale such as 1 to 10, with 10 preferred, and apply it as follows. Examine the alternative against a particular criterion—for instance, cost—and assign a unitless score from that scale. That is, choose the value on your 1-to-10 scale that best reflects the desirability of the cost of say, $425. Let us assume that you choose 8. Use this procedure for determining all criteria and all alternatives. The assigned rating should reflect the alternative's relative desirability. For example, the second procedure does the same thing: a little more effort yields greater accuracy. Because the second procedure is somewhat more involved, we postpone its explanation to a later section entitled, "The Second Procedure."

An example

This example centers on a store owner who faces making a decision about a garment rack. The alternatives are chrome, oak, and a style called "avant-garde." Using the steps given above, the owner identifies the criteria involved. Two are deemed essential: (1) cost must be under $500 per rack, and (2) holding capacity must be five or more garments per square foot or floor space. The owner continues by listing the noncrucial factors—attractiveness, compatibility with decor, durability, and delivery time. The owner next assigns weights to each factor, as shown in Table 8.3 (which gives the results of the process). A scale of 1 to 10 is chosen, with 10 representing the most favorable value. Note that this dictates that high numbers are preferred—an important consideration.

The avant-garde rack is eliminated because it does not satisfy the criterion of "capacity." We continue now to trace the owner's decision process.

The next step is assigning values for each criterion to each of the two remaining racks, chrome and oak. Again, a scale of 1 to 10 is chosen. When factual data is available, the task of assigning a rating is relatively easy. The owner expressed a preference for high numbers, yet low numbers are desirable when considering cost and delivery time. Caution in assigning ratings is required so as to reflect their desirability properly. With no other evidence, we must accept the owner's weights and ratings. The correctness of assigned ratings is usually debatable. Our purpose here is to understand the approach.

As reflected in Table 8.3, ratings are multiplied by the respective weights for the criteria and then summed for each alternative. The totals reflect a higher value for the oak rack; hence, it is the advisable choice.

TABLE 8.3: Weighted rating of three garment racks

Criteria	Weight	Chrome Rack			Oak Rack			Avant-garde Rack		
		Observations	Rate	Wtd Rtng	Observations	Rate	Wtd Rtng	Observations	Rate	Wtd Rtng
Essential										
1 Cost-must be less than $500/rack	10	$425 / rack	8	80	$390 / rack	9	90	$495 / rack		
2 Holding capacity must be at least 5 items per square foot of floor space	8	6 items per ft^2	7	56	5 items per ft^2	6	48	4.5 items per ft^2 *Reject*		
Desireable										
3 Attractiveness	6	modern but harsh	7	43	modern but warm	8	48			
4 Compatability with decor	8	OK	5	40	fits in well	8	64			
5 Durability	7	strong, but will scratch over time	5	35	strength: fair; but will scratch; can be refinished	4	28			
6 Delivery time	2	4 weeks	8	16	6 weeks	6	12			
Total	—	—	—	270	—	—	290			

The second procedure

The section entitled "Two Problem Areas" alluded to another way of rating against criteria, one designed to avoid values with units such as dollars or weeks. Below are instructions on how to do this.

Determine a unitless rating for each alternative by taking what is called a "ratio" of two values. Compare each alternative with the "best" by dividing one value by the other. If high numbers are preferred, put the best value on top; if low numbers are preferred, put the best on the bottom. Then multiply by 10 (if your scale goes to 10).

Admittedly, this sounds complicated; but it is not, as we will see. We return to the three racks. The least expensive rack—oak—is best if we consider only cost. Because high numbers are preferred, the price of the least cost rack (oak) is placed on top and the following is used to arrive at a rate for each rack:

$$\frac{\text{cost of least costly, or best, alternative}}{\text{cost of alternative being rated}} \times 10$$

To repeat, the costs are: chrome, \$425; oak, \$390; and avant-garde, \$495. Consequently, the ratings are:

chrome $\qquad \frac{390}{425} \times 10 = 9.2$

oak $\qquad \frac{390}{390} \times 10 = 10$

avante-garde $\qquad \frac{390}{495} \times 10 = 7.9$

Had you preferred low numbers, you would calculate the ratios with the "best" on the bottom. This approach yields ratings that accurately reflect the relative values of the alternatives. The ratio method is ideal for rating the holding-capacity and delivery-time criteria.

Impact factoring

In the example used to explain weighted rating, we did something subtle yet significant. The example places numerical values on "attractiveness" and "compatability with decor," intangibles generally considered nonquantifiable. Although the store owner did it, this is not always possible.

In contrast, the other criteria in the example are quite quantifiable. Cost is a criterion that is often quantifiable. Two others are capacity and delivery time; these are quantifiable in terms other than dollars.

The nonquantifiable factors that affect a decision can be, and often are, as significant as quantifiable factors. Nonquantifiable factors must be taken into account—but how, especially if we do not quantify them? The answer, is to recognize these factors, to assess them to the degree possible, and then incorporate them in a subjective (nonmechanical) decision-making process.

Impact factoring proves helpful here. Here it is helpful to adopt a different point of view. Our previous viewpoint was to establish criteria for a decision, to rate alternatives against the *criteria*. We could just as easily adopt the view that decision alternatives have *impact*. Choose an alternative, and you get its associated impact—for example, cost and compatibility (or incompatibility) with decor. The term *impact* is particularly appropriate in cases where nonquantifiable factors are significant. Impact factoring encourages the user to consider all relevant factors and to classify each factor as being either quantifiable in terms of dollars, quantifiable in terms other than dollars, or non-quantifiable. By doing this for each alternative, we can make a reasonable though less-than-scientific choice. An impact matrix helps here. The impact matrix is a general format used to guide an assessment of the impact of each alternative in a decision (see Fig. 8.4).

You may feel somewhat dissatisfied if left at this point. But little else can be said. The purpose of the matrix for impact factoring is to display the impact of decision choices. The best minds available have not yet developed a universally accepted approach to guide our decision process beyond the matrix point when nonquantifiables are involved. But with the matrix, you at least have before you a statement of the effect and impact of the decision confronting you.

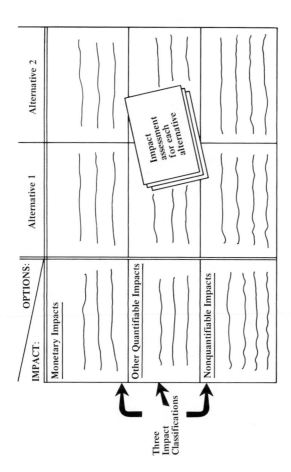

FIGURE 8.4: General form of matrix for impact factoring.

9

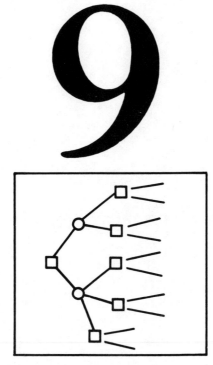

"Minie, Moe–"

OUTLINE
OF
CHAPTER
NINE

Checkers, Cards
and Life

DECISION
TREES

an example

form

value

steps

another example

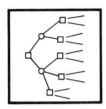

Checkers, cards and life

Some decisions are as easy to make as deciding whether to play checkers or cards. Being neither significant or complex, the decisions are made simply on the basis of the options before us. Other decisions, however, resemble those in actually playing checkers or cards. They take on a different complexion. Here, poor performance seems certain if we consider only our immediate options. The immediate move, we've learned, directly affects or restricts the subsequent move. Notice what checkers and cards do to us: these games force us to assess future decisions to make the present one.

In everyday life we face similar decisions. We are constantly making decisions. Often, the immediate decision, to some degree, affects subsequent decisions. What is the good move now? Often we know the answer only by evaluating future moves. Because this is difficult, good decision-makers sometimes use decision trees.

Decision trees

What is a decision tree? You may think of such a tree as a diagram of the way in which the future may unfold; each path is a different combination of your choices and the events of nature. You draw the tree to reflect decision alternatives, events that may occur, successive decisions, and the outcomes, or payoffs, that result from the first three.

An example

As an introduction to decision trees, consider the following situation. An employer concludes that he needs more staff because of his present workload. This calls for recruitment and selection. Positions will be advertised and applications taken. The question arises as to whether testing the applicants is worthwhile, given the cost involved and the possibility of holding interviews. Before the applicants can be tested, tests must be prepared or purchased. The employer seeks to clarify the advisability of this expense by drafting a decision tree (figure 9.1). To aid in your understanding the import of this tree diagram, we turn next to a discussion of the general format of decision trees.

Form

Decision trees have the general form shown in Figure 9.2. Time is construed as the present (on the left) and as the future (on the right). The tree consists of nodes (squares or circles) and branches (straight lines). Squares depict decision points. Lines emanating from the squares indicate decision alternatives. Circles with lines radiating to the right represent various possible events, or states of nature, that may result. When read from left to right, decision trees usually successively portray decision-event pairs. Finally, on the far right are outcomes, consequences, and payoffs for each decision path.

Among other things, a decision tree portrays the interplay of human acts and those of nature. Each linkage of branches, or paths, of the tree, each combination of personal choices and natural events, represents one way in which the future can unfold. Collectively the trees branches portray the various possible futures.

The tree aids your decision making to guide your choice of action toward a desirable future. From the tree you may prudently assess tomorrows decisions to make todays choices.

This situation is readily grasped in Figure 9.1. The first decision to be made is whether to test applicants. If the decision is not to test, the next decision becomes whether to interview applicants or to select them on the basis of their applications. On the other hand, if the employer tests the applicants, some may achieve high scores, though possibly none will. One future decision is whether to interview the high scorers. In the event of no high scorers, the employer may choose among the alternatives of recruiting applicants again, hiring a low scorer, or not hiring anyone.

How, then, does the employer decide on the best course of action— namely, whether to test or not? As you will see below, the tree is analyzed by working from right to left, evaluating successive decisions.

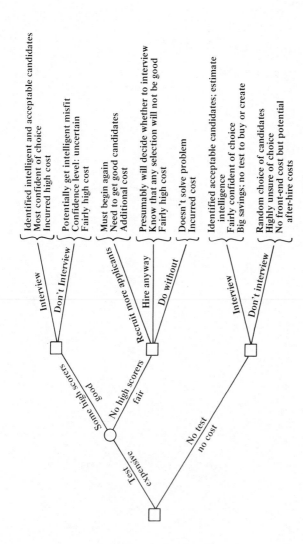

FIGURE 9.1: The employer's dilemma.

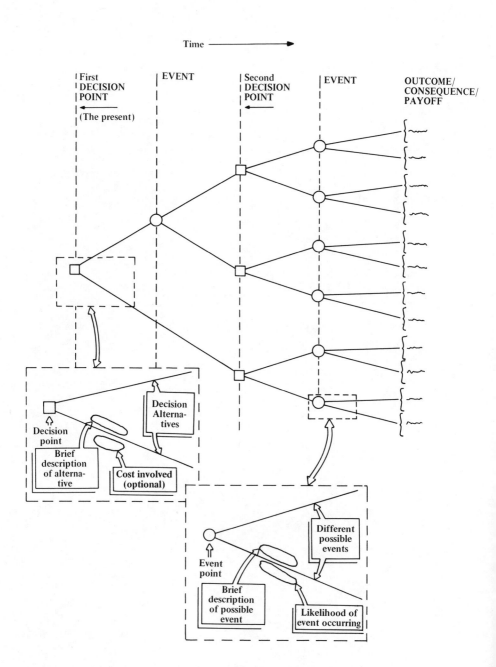

FIGURE 9.2: General form of Decision trees.

Below are outlined the steps in creating a decision tree and in analyzing the situation portrayed by the tree. The tree is created from left (to the right) and analyzed from the right (to the left).

Steps in creating a tree

Begin at the left with the first, or primary, decision. Label the alternatives and, if appropriate, indicate the cost associated with the alternatives.

To the right of each alternative, circle a node for events, if applicable. Denote possible events with radiating lines. It is sufficient to indicate only the major possibilities. Label each possibility above the line by describing it in a few words. Below the lines, label each possibility with an indicator of the likelihood of its occurring. You should be concerned with only one node at a time while doing this. The sum of all the possibilities for the various events from one circle node represents the total possibility of something occurring. Consider each node independently, without considering other event nodes in the diagram.

Continue developing the tree toward the right with as many decision and event nodes and lines as are appropriate for the particular situation.

On the far right, at the termination of each branch, denote the consequence or outcomes of the branch.

Analyzing the tree

The procedure involved is that of arriving at an informed decision by beginning with the farthest point in the future and working to the present. In doing this, place yourself at the right-hand termination of a branch representing a future. Assume that everything along the branch to the left has happened and is known.

Starting again at the far right, evaluate a given event node by looking at each event possibility and its outcome. Consider both the likelihood of occurrence and the outcome. Above the node, write in a number or descriptive word that summarizes the information of *all* events emanating from that node.

Do the same for each event that follows a decision node to the left.

Now you can assess the decision node on the immediate left of the event nodes summarized. Assume that you are now at that decision point, looking at those alternatives and the outcomes previously summarized. Choose the best alternative and X out the others.

Continue to work backward in time toward the present, in the fashion described above.

Another example

If you have read Chapter 4, you will recall the following situation. There you were asked to plan a symposium that was to begin in 45 days. A time-scale chart was used to define what was involved and to discover that 59 days were needed prior to the symposium for distributing the announcements and giving those invited time to respond. Yet a directive initially specified that the symposium was to begin in 45 days. To do so, however, presumably would limit the number of participants. Someone must make the decision whether to allow 45 days (and have fewer people) or 59 days (and have more people).

Something else was evident in the precedent diagram. Conference space has to be arranged within the first two weeks, to specify such in the announcements. Let us assume that two options exist for space—a large facility and a medium-sized one. Further, once made, the decision is essentially irrevocable. As the time for the symposium grows closer and you learn how many were actually planning to attend, you can not switch from one space to another. If you choose one space, the other will not be available; if you choose larger space, the cost will stay the same even for fewer people.

Let's assume that you are responsible for making the decision. You face two decisions that must be made soon: (1) early or late symposium, and (2) large or medium facility. How are you to make intelligent decisions? Yes, with a decision tree.

First construct the tree, drawing from the left the decisions and events as they occur. Here, in time sequence, occur two successive decisions, followed by consequences. The consequences arise from the decisions and events to their left. The resulting tree is shown in Figure 9.3.

The analysis begins at the right. The various possibilities and resultant outcomes of the top event node are examined. By weighing these likelihoods or outcome combinations, a general assessment is made, to summarize the top event node. For this node, the conclusion is one of negative, or adverse, result. In similar fashion, you successively evaluate each of the other rightmost event nodes, evaluating each node independently of the others. Recall that all elements on the left of a branch are assumed to have happened and to be known to you (see Fig. 9.4).

Having done this, you can now place yourself fairly easily at the decision points immediately to the left, and thus make the appropriate decisions for those points.

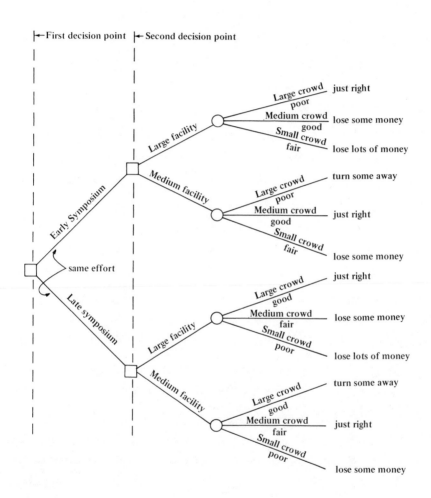

FIGURE 9.3: Symposium decision tree

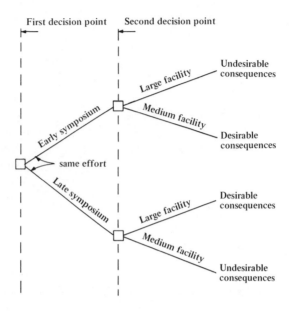

FIGURE 9.4: Symposium decision tree—reduced

You decide to reserve the medium facility for an early symposium, or the large facility if it is to be a late symposium. The second decision is thus made. But what about the first decision—that is, the first decision point? Should it be a late conference or an early one? The tree lays out the factors to help with the decision. The top, second decision node (at the second decision point) can be summarized as a "successful medium-sized symposium." The bottom, second decision node can be summarized as a "successful large symposium." Note that the cost, or effort required, is the same for either alternative, early or late symposium. All else being equal, you chose the late conference in order to get the most for your money. The decision is made: plan for a symposium to begin in 59 days, and reserve the large facility.

The power of decision trees is actually considerably greater than is described above. This is especially true of situations where the likelihood, cost, and outcome can be quantified. If this applies to you, see other references for guidance.

10

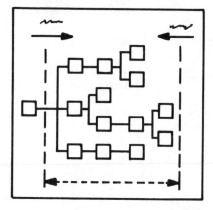

"Why Am I Here?"

OUTLINE
OF
CHAPTER
TEN
} Fast
Diagrams
{
A Fast INTRODUCTION { purpose
an example

FORM

GOALS, OBJECTIVES
AND TASKS

INTRODUCING AN EXAMPLE

STEPS

RETURNING TO THE
EXAMPLE
{ creating the diagram
the result
conclusion

POSTSCRIPT

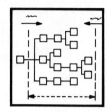

A FAST introduction

Following are three unrelated situations involving people. Based on personal experience, can you empathize with them?

Jack is committed to work toward a goal he believes in. Like many goals, his is a desired state that may never be achieved completely; but any progress is rewarding. Despite his convictions, Jack is frustrated by not knowing how to make the most of his efforts.

Suzanne is immersed in numerous tasks, all requiring attention and careful handling. Collectively, however, the tasks are confusing. All seem necessary, but their relationship and relative importance are not clear. Suzanne recognizes that this is what is undermining her control over her activities.

Vivian has informal supervision of three people, but a problem is evident. Although she herself is conscientious, the other three are not effective. By subtle inquiry, Vivian perceives that they do not understand why they must do what must be done.

Do any of these situations seem familiar? If they do, then you should know about FAST diagramming. FAST is an acronym for *functional analysis systems technique*. This versatile tool that lets you (1) plan how to reach your goals, (2) sort out numerous demands, and (3) structure meaning and purpose to your tasks. This is a large order, but FAST can help you achieve these goals in such a fashion.

Why *are* the three scenes familiar? Jack did not know how to get where he wanted to go; Suzanne didn't really know where she was; and Vivian's associates didn't know why they were there.

An example

Figure 10.1 is a reproduction of a FAST diagram encountered in Chapter 1. Although incomplete, it illustrates the principles involved. We begin the explanation of FAST with a discussion of its form; then an example is given.

Figure 10.2 shows the form of a FAST diagram. Figure 10.2a represents the background format and logic; the chart itself overlies the background. With one exception, the topics of concern lie entirely within the vertical dashes. How and Why take on meaning in Figure 10.2b.

FAST is applied to a particular situation, the elements of which are put in separate "boxes," thus forming the structure represented in 10.2b. Notice that, except for an element on the far left (the highest-order element), all elements fall within the dashed lines.

Pick any element, or box, and notice the directions under How and Why at the top. If you want to know *how* that element is to be accomplished, refer to the related elements to its right; if you want to know *why* the given element is important, look at the related element on the left.

Figure 10.2c is a more concrete example. Boxes are labeled G, O, and T, representing, respectively, goals, objectives, and tasks—three kinds of elements that are discussed below. G is the highest-order element, for it falls on the left of the dashed lines. How does one accomplish G? 10.2c focuses on one element (03) of four (in Fig. 10.2b, four elements are directly related to G). How does one accomplish 03?—By 05 and 06, as shown in Figure 10.2c. Conversely, why are 05 and 06 important at all?—Because achieving them helps achieve G. A FAST diagram depicts levels of hierarchy. Note that elements 05 and 06, for example, are on the same level, whereas 06 and T8 are not.

One more point must be made. You have undoubtedly observed WHEN on the right of the FAST diagram. If the sequence is relevant here, the relevance is implied by a vertical relationship of elements (for example, T8 before T9). Often, timing is not pertinent to the situation, hence no WHEN relationship is assumed among vertical elements.

Goals, objectives, and tasks

In some situations, users of FAST diagrams find it advantageous to use the words *goal*, *objective*, and *task* to distinguish between what are called *elements* above. Here we do not make much of the distinction. A

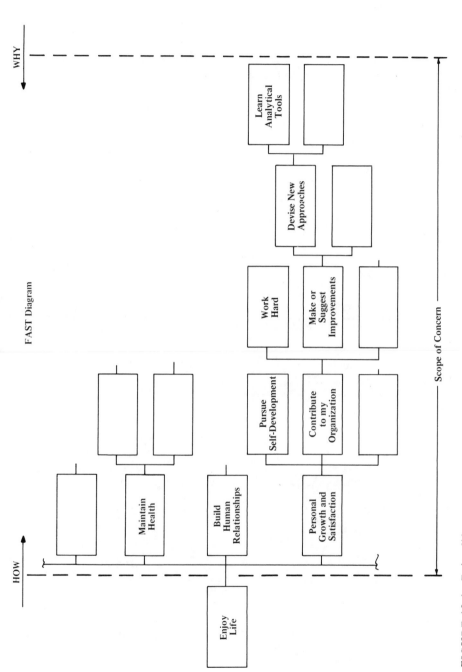

FIGURE 10.1: Enjoy life

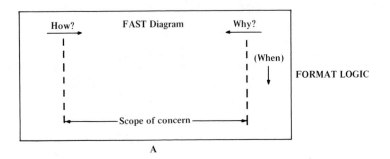

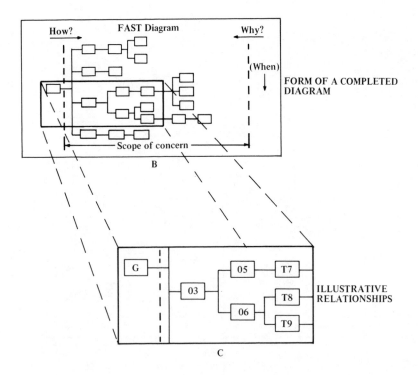

FIGURE 10.2: Form of fast diagrams

goal is considered a desired state, but one that is usually not wholly attainable—for example, eliminating hunger in cities. An *objective* is a more concrete, definable set of results to achieve a goal—for example, providing food to the urban needy. A *task* is a set of definite actions or work that one does to achieve objectives, such as distributing a thousand meals. Refer to Figure 10.2 for an example of how all three are involved: goals, objectives, and tasks. You should be able to classify each element as a goal, objective, or task. This distinction proves useful sometimes. In the following discussion of FAST, however, we will not make this distinction between the elements. Rather we shall concentrate on the chains of elements.

An example

The following situation will serve as an example throughout this chapter: A librarian wishes to guide the staff of a city branch library in creating a FAST diagram for the branch's activities. The purpose is to instill in everyone the relationship of the branch library's activities and the objectives the activities support. The librarian knows that once this is accomplished, it can serve as the basis for setting achievement levels for each objective. Thus the staff will know what is expected, and can help establish performance standards. This last part is discussed in Chapter 11. Their purpose, threrefore, is to create a FAST diagram for a library situation. Experience proves that the following steps can produce usable FAST diagrams.

Steps

1. If the situation described involves a group of people (for example, the library situation), have the group work together to create the FAST diagram.

2. First attempt to define the scope, or boundaries, of the situation to be examined; then keep the discussion focused within those boundaries. You may wish to change the scope later, but for now, define and stay within the scope.

3. "Brainstorm" the elements. That means verbalize as quickly as possible, the elements (goals, objectives, tasks, without distinguishing the elements as such). Write each down on separate cards and put it aside without evaluating study or concern over correct wording. Express each element in as few words as possible, e.g., simple verb-noun pairs.

4. On a blackboard or a large sheet of paper, prepare the format logic of the FAST diagram as shown in Figure 10.2a.

5. Construct the diagram by taping elements to the background format. Position the elements properly, so that their How and Why relationship makes sense. You will soon note the advantage of having each element on a separate card, as considerable shuffling is inevitable. Expect to change the wording of some elemets, discard other elements, and discover gaps in the logical relationship of some elements. For the last, expect to create new, previously unstated elements that will fill in the logic gaps.

6. When the diagram appears essentially correct, do two things. First, test the diagram by this method. For each and every element individually, ask the How and Why questions for that element, with respect to those elements on the right and the left. This way, inadequacies and inconsistencies will surface quickly. When the testing is complete, draw in horizontal and vertical lines on the background sheet that connect the elements and clarify their relationship. You now have, in rough form, a complete FAST diagram.

7. Finally, copy your diagram, making a clean FAST diagram in the size and presentation style desired.

Returning to the example

The librarian in our example assembles the staff and explains both the purpose of the gathering and the FAST-diagram technique. Initial brainstorming of library activities yields the following list:

- Check books in and out.
- Answer telephone inquiries.
- Process books for circulation.
- Keep circulation statistics.
- Attempt to satisfy user needs.
- Order new books.
- Catalog books.

- Help walk-in patrons.

- Organize check-out records.

- Classify new books.

- Keep library clean.

The group then begins the FAST diagram, using the list of elements. The preliminary result is shown in Figure 10.3.

The diagram is obviously inadequate; the elements are not tied together. When the group continues asking How and Why questions for the elements they have, many new elements become apparent. The final FAST diagram ties all the elements together (see Fig. 10.4).

Because the element, "satisfy user needs," is the highest-order goal, it is placed on the left. The element "keep library clean" is deleted as being extraneous to the scope of the diagram; all other elements are logically related. (Our library example centers on an existing function). Here, the staff began with elements on the right-hand side and added those on the left side. Do not infer this to be true for all situations.

Although the diagram clarifies the overall situation, is that all the diagram is useful for? No, it's not, since the librarian can use it further. For each element, starting at the left, the question can be asked, How do we know whether this has been accomplished well? This question leads to the development of criteria, or measures, for each element. Now the librarian has the beginning of a plan and a control system.

POSTSCRIPT

In this chapter we have mentioned placing the highest-order goal on the left of the veritcal line. The reasoning is as follows. Users of the FAST diagrams frequently employ the left vertical line to distinguish (by placing on the left of the dashed line) only those elements that they can *influence* from those which they can *control* (by putting them on the right). For example, the element "satisfy user needs" is one which the library staff can merely influence. In contrast, the three elements (build collection, provide check-out service, and answer reference questions) to the right of that goal (and to the right of the dashed line) can all be controlled. A significant difference exists between that which you can only influence and that which you can control.

Look to the next chapter for an extension of the library example.

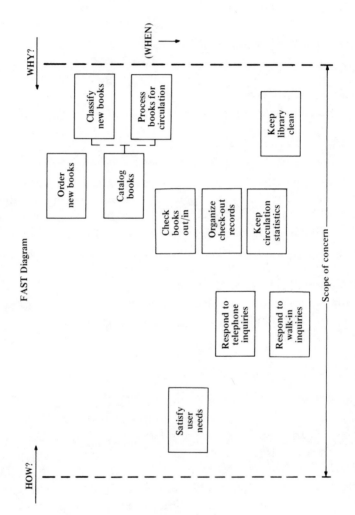

FIGURE 10.3: Library: initial effort

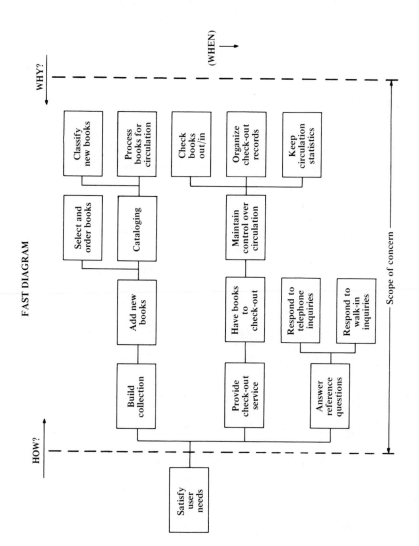

FAST DIAGRAM

FIGURE 10.4: Library: resulting diagram

11

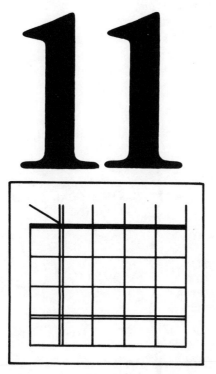

"This Is a GAS"

OUTLINE OF CHAPTER ELEVEN

GAS Means *GOAL ATTAINMENT SCALING*
- introduction
- value

A GAG for a GAS
- form
- an example

Steps
- planning stage
- evaluation stage

Another Example

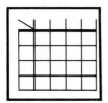

Goal Attainment Scaling (GAS)

Because you are methodical and know what you want, you state your goal. Rather than attempt to reach the goal in one leap, you do it in a series of steps, setting a series of objectives that, if attained, will lead to the goal. The effort required to achieve your goal becomes more manageable that way.

Managers have long recognized this principle, and attempt to set a reasonable, yet challenging, level of attainment for each of their objectives. Much has been written about this, but goal attainment scaling (GAS), helps to make all the theory practical. The technique developed by T. J. Kruiesuk and R. E. Sherman in the late 1960s, which, since that time, has found applicability in many public and social welfare programs. Because the technique contains the word *goal*, we use the word liberally in discussing the technique, dropping the distinction made in a chapter above between *goal* and *objective*. In this chapter the two words are used interchangeably, with no difference between the two intended.

In using goal attainment scaling, you lay out various objectives, assess the importance of each one, and—most importantly—establish various possible attainment level for each objective.

Why do this? We all know that, to get where we're going, it helps to establish a destination, or target. Yet, most likely, you will fall somewhat off your bullseye—a little lower or a little higher than expected. Targets usually have both the bullseye and the descriptors to help evaluate a hit. Goal attainment scaling is designed for you to assess your target and consciously evaluate, in advance, what constitutes great, expected, or poor goal attainment.

Form (GAG)

This will be explained by introducing a form and an example.

Using GAS, we state our goals and for each give several possible attainment levels, as described by some measure. A form called the goal attainment guide (GAG) is used in this process (Fig. 11.1). The form permits you to cite several goals, one per column, or, if you wish, to use the columns for different scales (or measures) that are to be applied to a specific goal. The body of the chart allows explicit statements of possible attainment levels. The bottom row provides a reference point, if an attainment level is applicable and is known for the present state, as it is now. Use this row only when it is relevant.

An example

To better understand this technique, consider an example based on the library situation in Chapter 10. There, the staff of a library recognizes the objective, "satisfy user needs." This goal necessitated three main objectives: (1) "build the collection," (2) "provide check-out service," and (3) "answer reference questions." Now assume that the librarian wishes to define these objectives more specifically in order to plan future performance. With the aid of the branch staff, the librarian uses GAG to scale the range of possible achievement levels (Fig. 11.2).

The entire staff can now identify and better understand the defined performance expectations of the library. (Later, we will discuss GAS for a particular individual.) Imagine the understanding that the staff might achieve if they had before them:

—the function of the library as portrayed in a FAST diagram
—the performance expectations as shown in a GAS chart
—the procedures of each library function documented as they might be with decision logic tables or some of the many kinds of flow charts

Each member of the staff could then see graphically the purpose of the work to be done, as well as the expectations that exist regarding the work and what processes must be employed to achieve the objectives set forth. Isn't that what most people need to fulfill their roles? But let us return to goal attainment scaling and examine the steps involved.

Goals listed separately

Brief goal statement expressed as a measure; Each given as a decimal; total overall goals to equal 1.0

For each level: brief qualitative description - or - range of values for the measure

Current level/situation (if known)

GOAL ATTAINMENT GUIDE

GOALS LEVEL of ATTAINMENT	#1 Relative Importance:	#2 Relative Importance:	#3 Relative Importance:	#4 Relative Importance:
MOST FAVORABLE OUTCOME THOUGHT LIKELY (+2)				
MORE-THAN EXPECTED (+1)				
EXPECTED LEVEL OF SUCCESS (0)				
LESS THAN EXPECTED (−1)				
HOST UNFAVORABLE OUTCOME THOUGHT LIKELY (−2)				
PRESENT (BASE) LEVEL				

FIGURE 11.1: Form of a goal attainment guide

GOALS / LEVEL of ATTAINMENT	#1 Build Collection by adding new books each month Relative Importance: .2	#2 Circulate books (complete cycle: check-out to reshelve) per month Relative Importance: .4	#3 Answer Reference questions (walk-in and phone) per month Relative Importance: .4	#4 Relative Importance:
MOST-FAVORABLE OUTCOME (+2) THOUGHT LIKELY	131–140	3201–3300 (average: 139–143/day)	1261–1380 (average: 55–60/day)	
MORE THAN EXPECTED (+1)	111–130	2801–3200 (average: 122–138/day)	1036–1260 (average: 45–54/day)	
EXPECTED LEVEL OF (0) SUCCESS	81–110	2401–2800 (average: 104–121/day)	806–1035 (average: 35–44/day)	
LESS-THAN EXPECTED (–1)	61–80	2201–2400 (average: 96–103/day)	576–805 (average: 25–34/day)	
MOST UNFAVORABLE OUTCOME THOUGHT (-2) LIKELY	51–60	2000–2200 (average: 87–95/day)	460–575 (average: 20–24/day)	
PRESENT (BASE) LEVEL (if known)	82	2520 (average: 110/day)	874 (average: 38/day)	

FIGURE 11.2: Goal attainment guide for a Branch Library

Steps

GAS has its value in two applications, planning (before something happens) and evaluation (after it happens). The steps are described separately for each application.

Planning

1. Decide on goals and objectives
   In this step, the utility of FAST diagrams prove very useful; see Chapter 10.

2. Weight the goals and objectives according to their relative importance

   Some will be more important than others. This should be reflected in the ranking. (Chapter 9 is helpful in this process by assigning each a weight according to its relative importance.) Assign each a decimal weight—for example, .1, .2, .3—where .2 indicates twice the importance of .1. The weights for all goals should total 1.0.

3. Select a criterion-measure scale (or more than one) for each goal— one(s) that would indicate goal achievement.

4. State the present—that is, current—level of goal achievement if it is known and is applicable.

5. For each goal, scale the achievement levels, using the goal attainment guide

   a. Begin with the center row, the expected level of attainment; then scale the higher and lower levels.
   b. If scaling by numerical value is possible (for example, number of books added), express the attainment level not as a singular target value such as 200 but as a range of values such as 150 to 250. Make the range of a level abut that of the adjoining level. That way, no matter what the outcome, the proper classification of attainment level will be clear.
   c. Where an objective cannot be expressed numerically, describe the attainment level with words as meaningfully as possible.

Evaluation

Goal attainment scaling proves useful in evaluating achievement after effort has been expended. Follow these steps.

1. Review the results and determine the appropriate achievement level for each goal or objective. Indicate, perhaps with a check mark, the cell describing the level actually attained. Do this for each goal or objective.

2. If an overall numerical value is desired (though this is not always useful), follow the procedure below.
   a. For each goal or objective, multiply the relative importance value (for example, .2) by the numerical value of the attainment level achieved (for example, 1). Here, the product is .2 x 1 = .2.

   b. Add the products for all goals or objectives. The result is a numerical assessment of the total performance. A value near zero indicates that the achievement was as expected; a positive value denotes a higher-than-expected total performance. Conversely, a negative value represents a lower-than-expected total performance.

Another example

We return to the library example. Assume that the librarian and an employee establish a GAS for that employee's work. Time passes. An assessment of the performance is made, and, to indicate this, achievement levels are indicated by check marks on the GAG chart (Fig. 11.3).

Our librarian wisely does not make the mistake of rating staff employees with overly simplistic, single-numerical values; no person or program of any size should be reduced to a number value. To do so can mislead more than it can clarify. Sometimes, however, it is useful to assess overall performance numerically—for example, as one among several evaluation devices. For our example, this is the result:

$$(+1 \times .3) + (0 \times .3) + (0 \times .3) + (+1 \times .1)$$
$$= .3 + 0 + 0 + .1$$
$$= .4$$

This positive number indicates a somewhat higher attainment level than was planned or expected.

GOALS LEVEL of ATTAINMENT	#1 Order new materials (books, magazines, etc.): purchase orders/month Relative Importance: .3	#2 Prepare new materials and catalog: items/month Relative Importance: .3	#3 Convert existing materials from Dewey to Library of Congress system: items/month Relative Importance: .3	#4 Maintain circulation statistics and organize check-out records Relative Importance: .1
MOST FAVORABLE OUTCOME THOUGHT (+2) LIKELY	21–25	231–276 (average: 10–12/day)	reference, biography and history sections	Both current and completely error free
MORE THAN EXPECTED (+1)	16–20 ✔	185–230 (average: 8–9.9/day)	reference, biography and half of history sections	Statistics current -and- few errors in check-out records ✔
EXPECTED LEVEL OF (0) SUCCESS	11–15	139–184 (average: 6–7.9/day) ✔	reference and biography sections ✔	Statistics fairly current -and- check-out records acceptable
LESS THAN EXPECTED (−1)	8–10	93–138 (average: 5–5.9/day)	reference and one-half biography sections	Behind in statistics -or- check-out records mis-filed
MOST UNFAVORABLE OUTCOME THOUGHT (−2) LIKELY	6–7	69–92 (average: 3–4.9/day)	reference section	Statistics incorrect or not done -and- check-out records disorganized
PRESENT (BASE) LEVEL (if known)	12	150 (average: 6.5/day)	—	Statistics fairly current -and- check-out records acceptable

FIGURE 11.3: Goal attainment guide for One Librarian

12

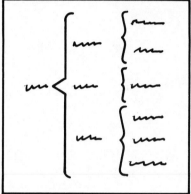

"Brace Yourself"

OUTLINE
OF
CHAPTER
TWELVE
{ WARNIER
DIAGRAMS

By Way of
Introduction . . .

The Basics { form
symbols
steps

Time-based Cycles

An Example

Value

Relationship to { FAST
Other Charts   ADP Flowcharts

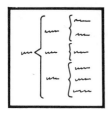

Warnier diagrams

Warnier diagrams are named for Jean-Dominique Warnier of France who invented them about 1970. In the United States they are more commonly known as Warnier-Orr diagrams, for Kenneth T. Orr, a leading American proponent of the tool who improved Warnier's concept.

We have already discussed Warnier diagrams. Each chapter of this book begins with a Warnier diagram. Think for a moment of what you have learned about these diagrams. They can depict sequence (an order of stated items is clear in each diagram) and hierarchy (explicit levels among the stated items are discerned visually). What about their utility, however? Reflect on your reaction to the diagrams. Did you find them useful? Clear? Self-explanatory? You probably answered yes to all three questions, and therein lies their value. Warnier diagrams may be viewed as word pictures, without being wordy.

What we have discussed so far, however, are stripped-down, light-weight versions of a high-powered construct.

The basics

The Warnier diagram portrays both the hierarchical and the sequential relationship of listed items, as an example see Fig. 12.1. Here, daily nutrition, breakfast, lunch, dinner are item names, or elements; breakfast, lunch, and dinner are subordinate to daily nutrition. The how-why relationship of the elements is clear. The fact that breakfast is above lunch denotes the sequence of breakfast before lunch. A similar position, or sequence relationship, denotes the sequence of lunch and dinner. In a Warnier diagram, one generates as many levels of hierarchy as needed.

159

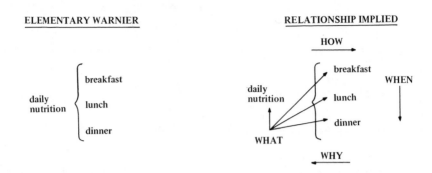

FIGURE 12.1

Add a set of symbols to the implications of the essential form above, and the Warnier diagram becomes versatile indeed. The symbols described below help portray sequence, repetition, and alternation. To understand these terms, consider $X \{ {y \atop z}$ where X, Y, and Z represent actions. We know that we do X by doing both Y and Z, with Y before Z. Depending on the situation, however, we may wish to repeat Y several times before doing Z. Or perhaps we wish to accomplish X by doing either Y or Z, but not both (concrete examples are given below). The above Warnier, as it stands, does not express either situation; so we augment the Warnier diagram with a set of symbols (Fig. 12.2).

To see each symbol in an application, refer to Figure 12.3. There, at the end of a week, two processes—payroll and production statistics are done (or can be done) concurrently. In payroll, for each employee, the actions taken are determined according to whether or not the employee is salaried. We assess the status of each employee, then execute the appropriate actions (once) for that employee. The actions are self-explanitory and are done sequentially. In production statistics, for each product we sequentially execute each described action once. If the actual payroll and production statistic steps (for example, subtract deductions) are stated, the above narrative would be considerably longer and more complex. Imagine how much clearer the Warnier diagram is than the narrative equivalent.

Steps

A little practice in drafting Warnier diagrams can be more beneficial than any statement of methodology about creating them. In constructing the diagrams, remember that (1) the hierarchy (high-to-low) goes

SYMBOL:	EXAMPLE:	MEANING:
{	Heading { Title / Date	Portrays a hierarchical relationship. Named item to left of brace is described by further detail to right of brace.
—	Employed	Means "not": negates named item below the bar. Read example as "not-employed."
( )	Shoot (1) or Shoot / Shoot (m)	Indicates repetition: quantity inside parentheses signifies number of times item is to be repeated. Top example: only once. Lower example: m times (where value of m is determined elsewhere)
+	Sell policies + Process claims	Denotes "concurrence"; that is, it infers that items above and below can occur simultaneously. (called "inclusive or") Read example as "sell and process concurrently." (*Without* the "+" a sequence is implied, i.e., example would be read "sell then process.")
$\oplus$	Approve ⊕ Disapprove or equivalently: Approve (0⊕1) ⊕ Disapprove (0⊕1)	Signifies "alternation," i.e., items above and below can not (or are not to) both occur, only one. (called "exclusive-or") Read equivalent examples as "either approve or disapprove (doing the chosen action only once)". (0⊕1) itself denotes "do (the element above this notation) zero or one times"

FIGURE 12.2

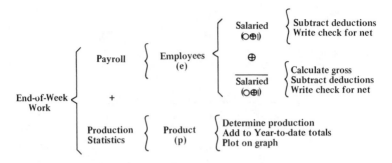

FIGURE 12.3

from left to right, and the sequence is implied at any level from top to bottom; and (2) the general approach is to develop the chart, working from the broadest viewpoint (or highest level, at the left) to the particular (successively to the right).

Time-based cycles

You will discover that many of our procedures and systems are based on time: actions are recurrently done at fixed periods. From daily feeding of the dog to preparing the annual federal budget, to some degree, we are governed by the clock. Thus, you should find time-based Warnier diagrams quite useful. Let me illustrate.

Consider an elementary Warnier diagram showing a "daily-hourly" time relationship: "daily" { "hourly" implies:

$$
\text{Daily} \left\{ \begin{array}{ll} \text{Start day} \\ \text{Hourly} \\ \text{End day} \end{array} \right. \left\{ \begin{array}{ll} X \\ Y \\ Z \end{array} \right.
$$

This can be interpreted as: Each hour of every day do X, Y, and then Z.

Imagine that we fill in a work report (WR) each hour, recording the type of work we are doing, and each day we punch a time clock (TC) or its equivalent. Our Warnier diagram would become:

$$
\text{Daily} \left\{ \begin{array}{ll} \text{Hourly} \\ \text{End day} \end{array} \right. \left\{ \begin{array}{ll} \text{Fill in (WR)} \\ \text{Punch (TC)} \end{array} \right.
$$

The concept is easily extended when and if periods are "nested", that is to say, one period precisely fits within another. For example.

or
Weekly	{	Daily	{	Hourly
Monthly	{	Daily	{	Hourly

We must be careful, though, to recognize when periods are not nested. For example, weeks do not fit precisely into months; only occasionally does a week begin when a month does. Consequently, we should *not* use the following expression:

~~{Monthly {Weekly {Daily {Hourly~~

Instead, the monthly-weekly-daily relationship is properly displayed in one of two ways: first, as though two separate yet concurrent procedures were involved

$$
\text{Monthly} \left\{ \begin{array}{l} \text{Daily} \\ + \\ \text{Weekly} \\ (0 \oplus 1) \end{array} \right. \qquad \{\ \text{Hourly}
$$

or as part of a single process

$$
\text{Monthly} \quad \{ \ \text{Daily} \quad \left\{ \begin{array}{l} \text{Start day} \\ \text{Hourly} \\ \text{End day} \\ \text{End week} \\ (0 \oplus 1) \end{array} \right.
$$

Thus we can express time relationships that are not nested.

Let us illustrate this framework. Imagine that an emoloyee is expected to:

—hourly fill in a work report (WR)
—at the end of each day, punch a time card (TC)
—at the end of each week, submit the WR
—at the end of each month, receive a paycheck (C)

The Warnier diagram for this is shown in Figure 12.4.

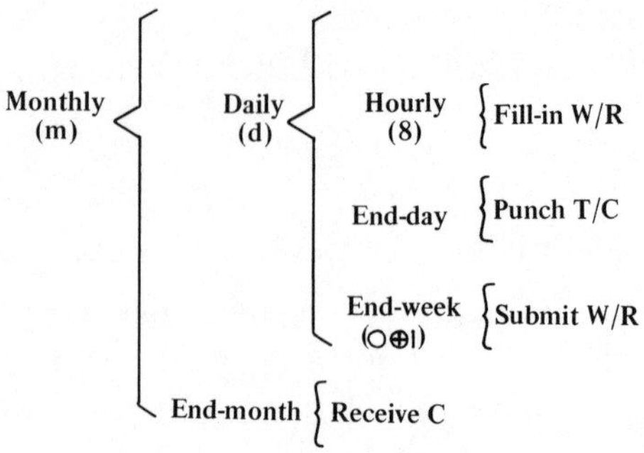

FIGURE 12.4

Time-based systems and procedures pervasively fill our lives. Using the above concept, you can describe any such situation, extending it to include biweekly, quarterly, semiannual, or annual periods. Be careful with relationships that are not nested. For example, annual-quarterly is a nested relationship, but quarterly-biweekly is not.

An example

Do you feel comfortable yet with Warnier diagrams? Or at least in interpreting them? Confirm your assurance with one more illustration. Figure 12.5 depicts "minimally required time-based nursing actions." Two abbreviations require clarification: *IV* stands for *intravenous* intake of medication, food, or fluids, whereas *I* and *O* denote the total fluid *intake* and *output* of a patient. Now test your understanding of a Warnier diagram by expressing the diagram in words.

As a check, compare your interpretation with portions A and B below.

A: These actions are to be taken for each 4-hour period (of which there are two in each shift). For each patient, the nurse must be concerned with both their vital signs and medication. The patient's vital signs are taken and recorded on a chart. If medication is required, it is first given to the patient and then the action is charted.

B: The required actions for each day are to be performed daily— namely, the requirements for each shift and the 4-hour periods of each shift. At the end of each day, for each patient, medical IV orders, if any, are renewed.

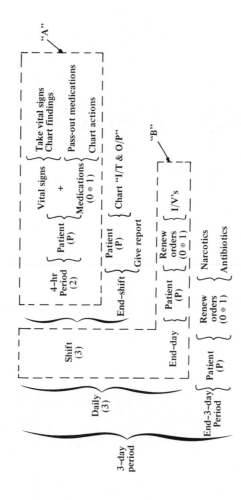

FIGURE 12.5: Minimally required time-based nursing actions.

Imagine that you supervise a nurse trainee, and that you may choose between a Warnier diagram and a written narrative of the entire set of actions. Which method of describing the required actions would you use to best train the nurse?

The value of the Warnier diagram lies in its use to design and to describe systems. Any logical structuring of information or actions can be called a *system*. For years the process of designing systems suffered for lack of logic tools. Warnier diagrams, a by-product of data processing field, have helped fill the void. Use this format to express your emerging thoughts as you design a system, no matter how large or small it may be.

The *description* ability of the Warnier diagram indicates its facility to portray the essential attributes of the hierarchy of order, both sequence and concurrence, repetition, and decision, or choice. One management consultant contends that Warnier diagrams "attempt to do too much." On the contrary, their value lies in the very ability to do so much.

Relation to other charts

By now you may have detected parallels between Warnier diagrams and FAST diagrams and ADP flowcharts. FAST diagrams and Warnier diagrams share the common why-how-what-when positional relation of their elements; in addition, Warnier diagrams are capable of expressing repetition and decision.

Warnier diagrams and ADP flowcharts both express sequence, repetition, and alternation, but through different pictorial mechanisms (FIG. 12.6).

Parallels between the charts exist, but so do differences. FAST diagrams do not express decision or repetition as do Warniers. ADP flowcharts do not differentiate hierarchical levels, unlike Warniers. Recognizing these distinctions will help your selection of the proper chart when you need one.